ODE TO JESUS

Also by Edward K. Watson

Is Jesus "God"? *A Witness to the World That Jesus is the Christ, the Eternal God* (in four volumes)

This is Jesus Christ: *An Interactive Aid to Understanding the Holy Bible's Core Message*

The Holy Spirit: *The God Within Us*

A Latter-day Saint Ode to Jesus: *The Most Influential Person Who Ever Lived*

Verifiable Evidence for the Book of Mormon: *Proof of Deliberate Design Within a Dictated Book*

The Iglesia Ni Cristo Under a Microscope: *Helping INC Members Keep More of Their Money, Survive Shunning, and Discover the Truth About Their Church and God*

Bliss: *A Guide for Women on Attracting and Keeping a Man*

Contentment: *A Guide for Couples on Maintaining a Great Companionship* (forthcoming, 2023)

The Adopted Children of God: *The Incomprehensible Fate of Christ's True Followers* (forthcoming, 2023)

10 Natural Rights: *Understanding Your Most Important Rights* (forthcoming, 2024)

How to Survive a Civilizational Collapse: *Baseline Survival Strategies* (forthcoming, 2024)

See www.edwardkwatson.com for more information.

ODE TO JESUS

The Most Influential Person Who Ever Lived

Edward K. Watson

Brainy-Press

Copyright © 2022 by Edward K. Watson.

All rights reserved. No part of this publication may be reproduced, stored in a retrieval system, or transmitted, in any form or by any means, electronic, mechanical, photocopying, recording, or otherwise, without the prior written permission of the author.

ISBN: 978-1-7779119-5-9

Cover image from Adobe Stock (136364712) Standard License. Cover design and all illustrations copyright © 2022, Edward K. Watson. Other photos and designs from Adobe Stock and Freekpik. Author photo copyright © 2022, Jeneffer M. Watson. All rights reserved.

Distributed by IngramSpark.

www.edwardkwatson.com

IMPORTANT!

1. All biblical quotations within ODE TO JESUS are paraphrased text and came from this author's four-volume IS JESUS "GOD"? (Brainy Press). A substantial portion of Part 1 and Part 3 are copied or derived from the same work.

   IS JESUS "GOD"? is a comprehensive examination of fifty-five (55) specific doctrines about Jesus that, when put together, shows the New Testament has a core message, a single soteriological cosmology centered on Jesus Christ. The work proves that the New Testament is a *frameless, unharmonized, correlative anthology* — an astonishing accomplishment without parallel in literature. This is the only empirical evidence that gives a very high probability that something supernatural was involved in the New Testament's creation.

2. This book uses "Jesus," "Christ," "Jesus Christ," "the Son of God," and "the Son" interchangeably.

The Holy Bible's Core Message or "Gospel"

God's only Son, JESUS CHRIST, the Creator of the universe who is "God" by nature – obeyed his Father's will and became human flesh. He then suffered and died to annul the Fall – when Adam and Eve transgressed and inflicted sin, death, moral weakness, and trials on humanity.

He rose from the dead to destroy death itself and make all humans immortal physical beings. He will then judge all humankind at the Last Day according to our works.

He conjoined the divine and human natures so that his grace allows some humans to be "adopted" by God, share ultimate glory, and participate in God's very nature, mutual indwelling, and oneness.

All who come unto JESUS CHRIST, repent of their sins, get baptized in his name, strive to live his teachings whereby the Holy Spirit within them continually refines and purifies them, and endure to the end will be rewarded with eternal bliss in his kingdom.

Table of Contents

INTRODUCTION 1

    Book Layout 4

    True Biblical Doctrine and Interpretations are not the Same 5

PART 1: CREDIBILITY OF JESUS AND THE HOLY BIBLE 11

    Jesus Made Your Life Tangibly Better 13

    How to Know That the Bible is Credible 40

    Strive to Become One of the Glorified and Exalted Children of God 48

    My Witness 51

PART 2: ODE TO JESUS HYMNS 53

    Prologue 54

    1. The Pre-Existence of Jesus 56

    2. Jesus Mutually Indwells With the Father 60

    3. Jesus is the Almighty Creator 64

    4. Jesus Became Human 68

    5. The Atonement of Jesus 72

    6. The Resurrection of Jesus 76

    7. The Glorification of Jesus 80

    8. Jesus Creates the Children of God 84

Epilogue 88

PART 3: HYMN STANZA CLARIFICATIONS 91

Methodology 93

Clarification of the "Prologue" Stanzas 96

Clarification of the "1. The Pre-Existence of Jesus" Stanzas 106

Clarification of the "2. Jesus Mutually Indwells With the Father" Stanzas 136

Clarification of the "3. Jesus is the Almighty Creator" Stanzas 146

Clarification of the "4. Jesus Became Human" Stanzas 151

Clarification of the "5. The Atonement of Jesus" Stanzas 162

Clarification of the "6. The Resurrection of Jesus" Stanzas 168

Clarification of the "7. The Glorification of Jesus" Stanzas 176

Clarification of the "8. Jesus Creates the Children of God" Stanzas 187

CONCLUSION 199

SCRIPTURE REFERENCE GUIDE 203

Old Testament 203

New Testament 206
INDEX 217

List of Tables

Table 1: Jesus is God 108

Table 2: Jesus is Jehovah..126

INTRODUCTION

Ode to Jesus is the easiest way for you to learn the Holy Bible's real teachings about Jesus Christ. In mere *seconds*, you will know what it says about the most influential person in history. It does this by using hymns that benchmark true biblical doctrines in an easily remembered and understood way. For instance:

God made the universe through Christ.

Sire ordered; Son obeyed!

This reality came to be –

Father designed; Son made!

Just like that, you now know a critical biblical teaching: God the Father had his Son, Jesus Christ, create this massive universe. Here is another:

He humbled himself to be born.

The great God became man!

He emptied himself of glory.

From divine to mere man!

In like manner, you now know that the Bible teaches God (Jesus) humbled himself and gave up his glory to become human.

> *Christ's Atonement was infinite.*
>
> *Pain, inconceivable!*
>
> *It was infinite hurt and fear.*
>
> *Unimaginable!*

You now have an idea of the magnitude of Christ's physical and mental suffering when he took upon himself the consequences of all the sins of all humans for all time.

> *Christ makes everyone immortal –*
>
> *Both righteous and flawed!*
>
> *This bequest he gives to us all.*
>
> *In our flesh, we'll see God!*

In the few minutes that you have been reading this book, you now possess true biblical knowledge that makes it impossible for someone to deceive you on the subjects covered by the sample stanzas. You are now equipped with the Bible's standard and can determine whether a belief accurately aligns with its actual teaching. And if you take the time to examine the referenced passages of each stanza in Part 2 and the deeper dive in Part 3, you will validate that the Bible really does teach those doctrines.

What you do with the knowledge is up to you. You can use it to believe the Bible's message and live a life of meaning and joy by becoming a person who loves God, loves your neighbor, loves yourself, and keeps God's commandments. Alternatively, you can restrict it to the intellectual satisfaction realm. But regardless of your choice, at least now, no one can fool you about what the Bible actually says about Jesus Christ.

Jesus Christ will return to earth.

He will come suddenly!

With angels and the righteous dead.

With great might and glory!

This book attempts to counter the confusion, intolerance, and fear that occur when people and cultures lose their moral foundation. If you let it, *Ode to Jesus* grounds you on what is truly important in life. Regularly reading or singing the hymns lets you feel the Holy Spirit comfort you since he testifies of the Son of God. Read and ponder the hymns if you are feeling down or struggling to overcome a trial. Look up the referenced passages and read them in context. Allow the Word of God to strengthen you and keep you on the right path.

You have within your hands the means to finally grasp just how monumental Christ's teachings were and how Christianity changed the world and improved everyone's lives.

Jesus shares all he has with us –

For those who stay faithful!

Those who endure will rule with him –

A gift so wonderful!

Book Layout

Ode to Jesus has three parts and starts by explaining why Jesus Christ and the Holy Bible are credible. Virtually everything that makes your life worth living owes a debt to Jesus because his followers established the modern-day world, with its natural rights, representative governments, the rule of law, capitalism, and modern Science, Technology, Engineering, and Mathematics (STEM). Even more important is the brilliance of Christ's words that, when applied, directly result in having a meaningful life. It examines Christ's infinite Atonement – the single most impactful thing that has ever happened, and issues an invitation to take charge of your life by deliberately choosing the hard path.

Part 2 is the heart of the book, which is the hymns. It contains eight core hymns that are bookmarked by a prologue and epilogue. Each hymn is comprised of eight stanzas that share a common theme. Immediately after the stanzas are the scripture references for each that validate the stanza's main doctrine.

Part 3 provides more details about each hymn. It examines each stanza and includes a representative passage that shows the concept is clearly found in the scriptures.

True Biblical Doctrine and Interpretations are not the Same

This book is only concerned with what the Holy Bible says and allows it to speak for itself without placing a theological lens over the text. The natural, *prima facie* or face value meaning of the text is assumed to be the default understanding instead of letting a theology override the simplest, literal reading.

> *This book defaults to the face value phrasing of the text to understand its meaning even when the expressed idea differs from how it is typically understood.*

It is critical to treat the biblical text this way because the phrasing of the text is "doctrine," but the explanation of what it means is "interpretation." These are not the same thing. The expressed doctrine does not change, but interpretations have no end – every person can have their own. Failure to recognize the difference leads to conflict, confusion, and possible loss of eternal life.

You and I can read the same scripture text but understand it differently. And that is perfectly ok because we are human, not tools that only function using just one low-level machine language code. Your perspective could be right, and my opposing viewpoint could be wrong, or mine is right and yours is wrong, or both of our points of view may be wrong. But the expressed doctrine—the phrasing of the scripture text itself—stays firm.

For instance:

"Do you not believe that I am in the Father, and the Father is in me? The words I say are not from me but from the Father who dwells in me. 11 Believe me when I say I am in the Father and the Father is in me or at least believe because my work. . . 20 On that day, you will understand that I am in my Father, and you are in me, and I am in you." (Holy Bible: John 14:10-11,20)

According to the Holy Bible, Jesus is in the Father and the Father is in Jesus. This is official Christian doctrine, and it cannot be understood to mean the opposite of what it says (i.e., it will never say Jesus is *not* in the Father nor that the Father is *not* in Jesus).

How we reason out or understand the divine mutual indwelling and oneness found in John 14:10-11,20 is "interpretation." And the interpretation could be true, partially true, partially false, or entirely false. But even if our interpretation were completely false of a doctrine that we accept, especially if the doctrine was abstract and we have no frame of reference for it, the worst that could happen to us when standing before Christ to be judged is the recognition that we misunderstood the doctrine's meaning.

> *If interpretations of abstract ideas mattered to God, then why did he not clarify in the Holy Bible <u>how</u> the abstract ideas should be <u>understood</u>? A just and loving God cannot condemn us for failing to understand something he gave no indication was important to be understood in a specific way, especially when they conflict with what he did tell us was critically vital to our eternal fate.*

Here is what we do know:

> *God does not care for what is in your head. Neither does he care about your persuasion skills, wealth, education, beauty, physique, color, race, gender, or popularity. What he cares about is on what you <u>become</u> during your brief time in mortality. Did you grow into a person who loves God, loves your neighbor, and loves yourself? Did you strive to keep his commandments?*

God's main evaluation criteria when he judges us is whether our *behavior* aligned with his nature and commandments since true belief is always behavioral; his genuine followers live in a particular way that demonstrates their belief.

Behavior is always more important than interpretation.

The risk lies when we insist that our personal interpretation is the only possible explanation for a doctrine.[1] This risk escalates into outright danger to our salvation if we use it to judge others and threaten them with eternal damnation for refusing to believe our specific interpretation.

Such actions show a lack of charity to the fact that God gave humans the freedom to believe or not believe according to our own conscience and we have the innate right to interpret scripture however we want. Our freedom of thought is the most basic of rights; it is the core of what it means to be human. Even the most oppressed slave is free to think whatever he wants.

If God never insisted that we interpret a scriptural passage in a specific way to be saved, then no one else has the right to demand that we comply with their interpretation to be saved.

Uncharitable dogmatists attempt to replace God's authority over us, but Jesus Christ, alone, has judgment authority over humankind. No one can force him to obey their will and condemn people to eternal damnation just because they think the "unbelievers" ought to be

---

[1] Since interpretation is subjective, it is vital to try to see things from the perspective of others. There are credible reasons why intelligent, good people can read the same passage but understand it differently.

condemned for refusing to agree with a specific interpretation. Christ was very clear:

You will be judged with the same standard that you judge others; you will be measured with the same measure you use on others. (Matthew 7:2)

Only Jesus Christ has the right to judge us as he is the only one who sees our innermost secrets and thoughts. Any uncharitable behavior toward others will be applied in equal measure against the perpetrator when it is their turn to be judged by Christ.

Christ's primary concern is for us to voluntarily grow while mortal into beings of love so that when we die, we can unite with the God of love (1 John 4:16-17). Those without charity will not receive charity when they are judged and will miss out on sharing God's nature, oneness, and glory.

Consequently, ignore those who usurp God's authority by telling you that you must interpret or understand biblical passages in a specific way to be saved, especially on abstract ideas that God never elaborated. God made you free. You are free to grow and learn in your own way and at your own pace. And if your interpretation changes over time (as it typically does for most of us), then that is perfectly fine too. Just stay the master of your own mind and prioritize what God cares about, which is <u>*behaving*</u> as his true follower.

Become a person of love, and you will be thrilled when it is your turn to stand before him.

So, come. Join me in singing and having joy in Jesus Christ for who he is and all he did for us!

PART 1: CREDIBILITY OF JESUS AND THE HOLY BIBLE

Jesus Made Your Life Tangibly Better

It is impossible to exaggerate your debt to Jesus Christ – even if you do not believe he is our God and Savior. His ideas revolutionized how we view ourselves and others. His moral teachings resulted in our "inalienable" natural rights,[2] and those influenced by his teachings established the legal mechanisms to defend these rights. Christians and others who believed in the Christian worldview also created the nations of Europe and North America, which

---

[2] From a moral standpoint, we have reciprocal natural rights – rights that are inherent in us as humans and do not come from any government. Consequently, they cannot be morally taken away by anyone, provided we do not violate the natural rights of others or break the social contract (where we knowingly and willingly subject these rights to a human law). Natural rights are "human rights" that do not need the government or money to enforce. They apply to everyone equally.

Because we are human, we have a natural right to:

1. Life
2. Liberty
3. Physical Security
4. Fair Trial
5. Equality
6. Property
7. Freedom of Religion
8. Pursue Happiness
9. Freedom of Speech
10. Vote for a Representative Government

are directly responsible for today's technological world and all its benefits. They established and nurtured modern STEM, capitalism, the rule of law, and representative governments – all of which vastly improved the human condition. In addition, they influenced other nations and cultures, sometimes by force, to respect the natural rights of their citizens and those of other countries.

> *We cannot overstate Jesus Christ's impact for good on the world. Every person today is positively affected in one way or another by ideas and products that can be shown to owe a debt to Jesus and his followers.*

Christ's Teachings Directly Resulted in Your Natural Rights

When the framers of Western civilization were creating the modern nations of Europe and North America, they needed a set of governance rules and a judicial system for each nation that replaced the absolute monarchy models of the past.

The Americans were the first to recognize the supremacy of natural rights, which they enshrined in the US Constitution in 1789. As the new country's supreme law, it became the foundation for transforming society into one where a person's natural rights took precedence over human law. As the nation matured and more Americans wanted natural rights for those who were enslaved, the US went through the Civil War, which saw the freeing of the slaves and the loss of power by those wanting to continue the old order.

For the most part, the Europeans ignored following the Americans in enshrining natural rights into their supreme laws despite accepting some in reduced form. But their attitude changed after the devastating wars of the 19th and especially 20th centuries, which killed a sizable percentage of their population, destroyed their economies, and reduced great swaths of the continent to rubble.

The American success in unifying a continent and the material success of its people became something to be admired and emulated. Thus, the Europeans now imitated the Americans in recognizing the natural rights of those within their borders to various extents.

The result of copying the Americans was astonishing! The Europeans experienced the longest period of peace and the greatest increase in the quality of life in their history. Industries, militaries, and economies were shared, judicial codes were standardized, and national borders could be traversed without stopping.

The West's success became an example for the rest of the world. The nations that enshrined natural rights into their governing and judicial systems leapfrogged economically and socially ahead of those that did not.

The benefits of recognizing natural rights are obvious today, but where did the idea that we have these rights come from? Where did the US Founding Fathers like George Washington, Benjamin Franklin, Thomas Jefferson, and James Madison get the transformative idea of natural rights?

If a right isn't reciprocal, then it isn't a natural right.

The idea that humans have natural rights come from Jesus Christ's teachings. Some of these are:

"Do unto others what you want to be done to you." (Matthew 7:12)

"Whatever you did to the most unimportant of my brothers and sisters, you did it to me ... Whatever you did not do to the most unimportant of my brothers and sisters, you did not do it to me." (Matthew 25:40,45)

"Love your neighbor as you love yourself." (Mark 12:31)

"Love one another." (John 13:34)

"There is no Jew or Gentile, slave or free, or male or female: You are all one in Christ Jesus." (Galatians 3:28)

These teachings of empathetic morality, human equality, and the innate dignity of all humans are ideas that the US Founding Fathers have known since childhood. These moral principles framed their outlook on interpersonal relations and are the direct source of the concept of natural rights.

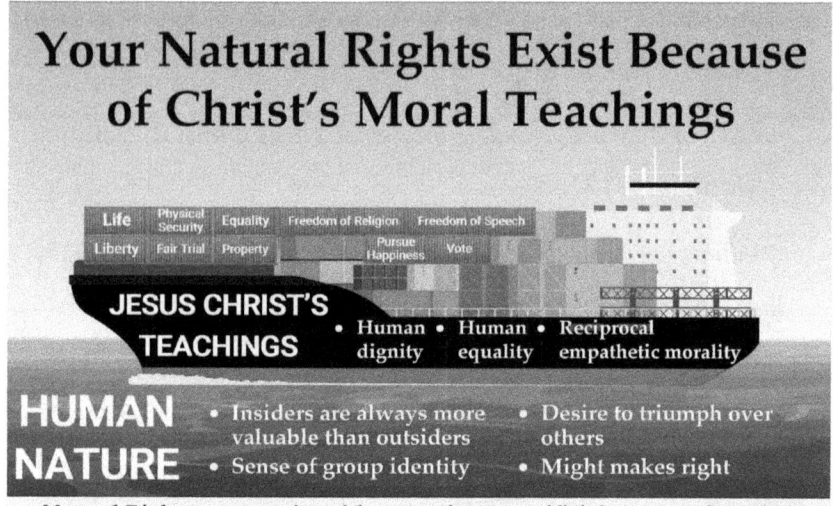

Natural Rights cannot exist without resting on artificial support since they violate human nature. Remove Christ, and these rights disappear into the depths of our nature because nothing *objective* justifies them.

Societies that applied Christ's moral teachings became the most attractive in history. Serving God meant having genuine love and charity toward others. It meant serving each other and taking responsibility for the welfare of others. It meant swallowing one's pride and tolerating differences. Moral discipline (the action of obeying rules and doing "good") and bodily self-control (the deferment or rejection of selfish pleasure) became <u>*internal*</u> instead of externally enforced by the state or by another authority figure.[3]

---

[3] For example, the true follower of Jesus Christ does not keep the money they saw fell out of a pocket of an "enemy" because their internal moral code tells them that it is "wrong." They do not need to

So thoroughly has the West absorbed Christ's morality into our culture's ethics that most believe we possess inherent rights and assume that recognition is standard everywhere. Even atheists who argue against belief in God assert that Christ's Golden Rule ("Do unto others what you want done to yourself") is innate within us – that we do not need God to be "good."

But these are simply untrue.

Our core human nature prioritizes insiders over outsiders. This is why we will always save our young child's life over a stranger's a hundred times out of a hundred. This explains why a tragic death in our neighborhood affects us more than one that happens in a distant land. Our sense of group identity is responsible for most of the violence and brutality that our species commits. This explains why nations go to war against other nations even if they share the same religion; their national group identity supersedes their religious identity. Our internal desire to triumph over others, especially when having power, explains why people in

---

be externally forced by the state to return the cash on pain of punishment.

It is that internal moral code that made the West the most attractive and successful civilization in history.

positions of power tend to want to keep that power or even extend it. Thus, tyrants and those with weapons victimize the helpless.

But even those who believe we have natural rights disagree on where the rights start and end. For instance, countries as close as Canada and the United States diverge on whether a specific act is moral or immoral. This discrepancy is even worse when comparing Western and non-Western nations. One only needs to live outside the West to see that nations do not share the same values.

Christ's teachings changed us as a species. Those who internalized his teachings of human dignity, equality, and reciprocal empathetic morality created something the world has never seen before:

Natural rights.

The paradigm that recognizes everyone, even our worst enemy, has natural rights equal to our own counters humanity's default nature that "might makes right" and "powerful insiders are more valuable than weak outsiders."

> *Applying Christ's teachings creates an <u>artificial</u> floor to our values that prevent us from plunging into our fundamental nature that is cruel and unfair to others.*

Following Christ's moral principles establishes civil societies that are attractive and enjoyable to live in. When enforced by the state as a rule of law that applies to all equally, these principles create the best of all possible worlds: People can enjoy living within safe communities that give equal opportunity for the pursuit of happiness, and where differences are tolerated when they do not trample on the natural rights of others or violate the social contract that the community knowingly agreed to follow.

The overwhelming social benefit of Christ's moral teachings explains why people everywhere changed their societies to give their citizens equal rights. Nations that refused stagnated and experienced brain drains of their best and brightest, who went to places where they could live where their natural rights were respected.

We must never lose sight of the source of the West's human ethics: **The teachings of Jesus Christ**. Without this foundation, the ethics have no objective justification.

For example, where did atheists get the idea all humans have equal worth regardless of race, wealth, social status, appearance, and sexual orientation? Who told them this is "good" and its opposite is "evil"? The idea is not self-evident in nature or outside Christian morality. As Burke and Bentham pointed out way back in the 18th century, "inalienable natural rights" is an idea that floats on air because it cannot be validated by anything objective. This explains why no religion or philosophy in history taught it before Christians started creating the modern West.

It is easy to demonstrate the problem of inalienable natural rights when ignoring Christian morality by asking atheists and other anti-Christians:

- Why is slavery wrong, and who told you that you have a right not to become a slave?
- Why is it wrong for you to be tortured?
- Why is racism wrong, and who told you all races are equal?
- Why is it wrong to force someone to join a religion and who told you that you have freedom of religion?
- Why is wife-beating wrong, and who told you women are equal to men?

The immediate answer is "the law" or "the government." But where did the government come up with the ideas, and what justified them? When one traces the ideas back, they all lead to Christ's moral teachings such as his Golden Rule that the framers of the West internalized. That was when humanity's values cleaved, creating a new path that recognized natural rights for the first time in history.

CREDIBILITY OF JESUS & THE HOLY BIBLE | 23

To say it another way:

How does the unbeliever justify the belief that humans have innate worth and equality when these ideas contradict human nature's core value that powerful insiders are more valuable than weak outsiders?

Because Jesus Christ said so.

The most virulent anti-Christian directly benefits from ideas that are not just derived from Christ but are actively sustained and supported by his teachings. Remove the source, and the concept of natural rights collapses because nothing objective justifies them except Christ's words.

The biological fact that all humans belong to the same species is <u>irrelevant</u> since humanity's default nature always places greater value on insiders than outsiders.

This explains why slavery historically existed everywhere and why people have been killing "outsiders" since we lived in bands and tribes. You will always save your young child's life over a stranger's; you would not be human were it not so.

Those who try to extinguish Christianity and its influence in our world are like a man hammering away at a building's foundation. If he succeeds in his goal, the building will collapse, crushing him and everyone else inside it.

Any attempt to remove the West's Christian foundation eliminates the validation of our innate worth and equality. Standards then become arbitrary and changeable on the whim of whoever is in charge. Tyranny returns, resulting in calamity for the rest of us.

Good people everywhere, Christians and non-Christians, must oppose any attempt to weaken our civilization's foundation but underpin it instead. Christ's words are too valuable to ignore.

Christ's Teachings Directly Led to the Modern World With All Its Benefits

Slavery was normal in virtually all human societies for thousands of years but is now gone except in a few places. Why?

For thousands of years and in nearly all societies, women were the property of their fathers and then husbands. So what explains the drastic change in the status of women in "civilized" nations?

Pedophilia was normal everywhere, where adult men had sexual relations with children below what is now the "age of consent." So why is it considered one of the worst evils today by all good people?

The answer is Jesus Christ. His moral teachings influenced us to enact laws that made our world tangibly better.

But this is not all. We now enjoy property rights, electric grids, highway infrastructure, water and wastewater systems, hospitals, public schools, universities, medicine, the internet, and much more. And all of these are direct results of Christ's followers living in a capitalist environment that recognized their natural rights (such as property rights), allowing for the emergence of modern Science, Technology, Engineering, and Mathematics (STEM).

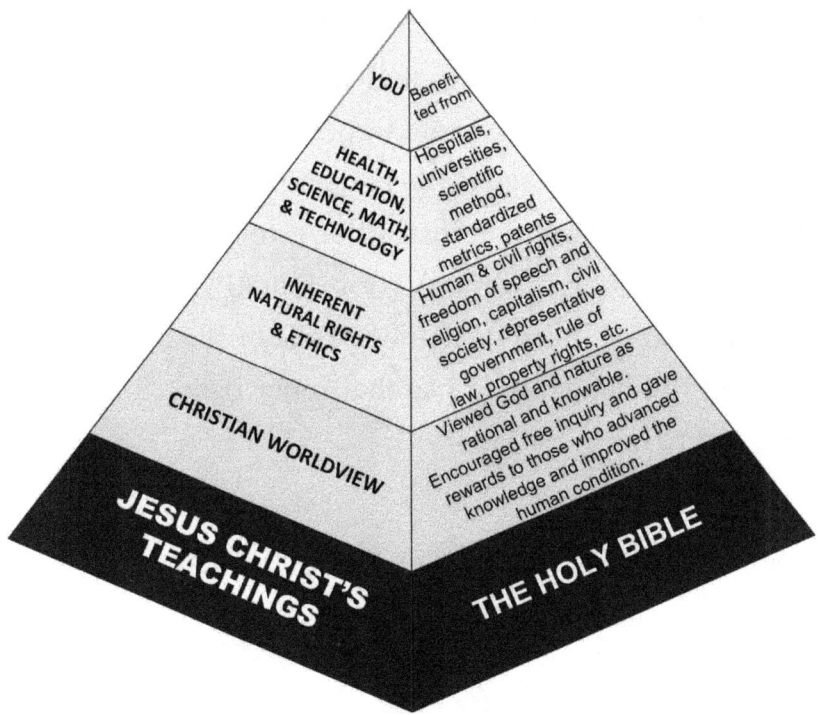

The West has dominated the world for the past five centuries because any culture that attempts to live according to Christ's teachings of empathetic morality, human equality, and the innate dignity of all humans leverages the human drive to succeed when people materially benefit from their labor and creativity.

These facts should give any Christian immense joy and gratitude for being a Christian. Even today, millions migrate to nations founded on Christian principles to give themselves and their children better lives and futures. Actions always speak louder than words.

Christ Taught Us How to Live a Life of Meaning and Joy

Of all the *tangible* benefits that Jesus Christ's teachings gave humanity, none is more important than living a life of meaning. It supersedes the recognition of your natural rights since it is internal instead of external. It speaks to who and what you are. Viktor Frankl[4] and Richard Wurmbrand[5] showed us that even an abused slave could live and die happy if he has that inner peace that gives meaning to his life.

---

[4] See Frankl, V. *Man's Search for Meaning.*
[5] See Wurmbrand. R. *Tortured for Christ.*

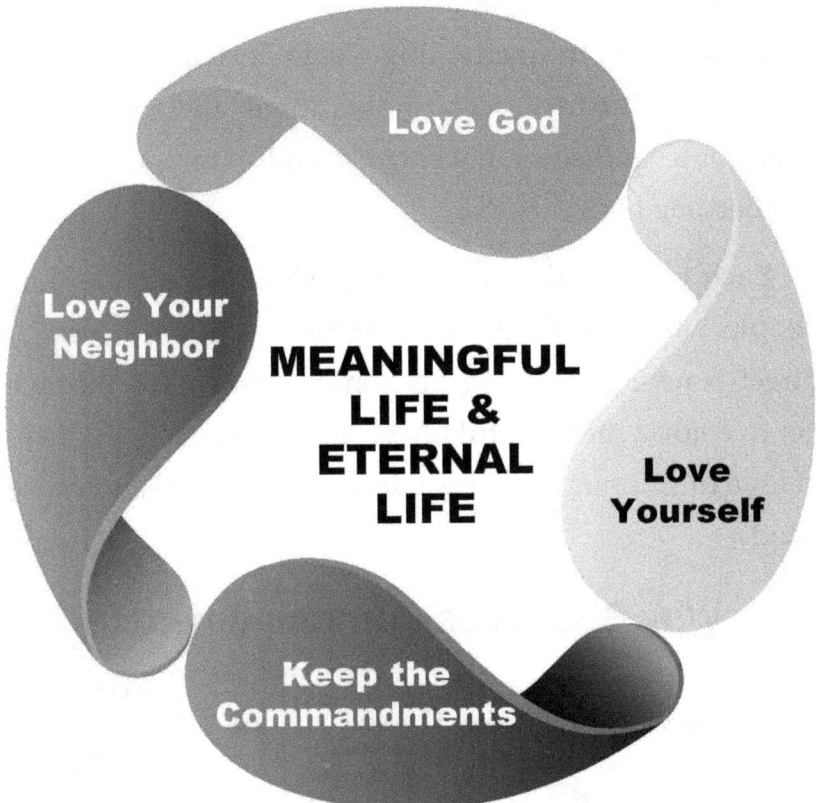

If you apply Jesus Christ's teachings of loving God, your neighbor, and yourself while striving to keep his commandments, you are <u>guaranteed</u> to find joy and contentment with your life regardless of all evil and pain you experience. You will die happy since you made a positive difference to humanity, and *used your time on earth to become a person of love and become <u>identical</u> to the God of love* (1 John 4:16-17).

Keeping God's commandments is critical to having a meaningful life because they benefit us, not God. He does not need us to worship him. Neither does he gain strength or nourishment from anything we do. Instead, God gives us commandments because he loves us and wants to adopt us and share his oneness and nature so that we can become his heirs.

Each commandment is designed to help us become people who love God, our neighbor, and ourselves. A direct benefit of keeping his commandments is that we get to enjoy a meaningful life because becoming a person of love fulfills our innermost desires to be good and cause good.

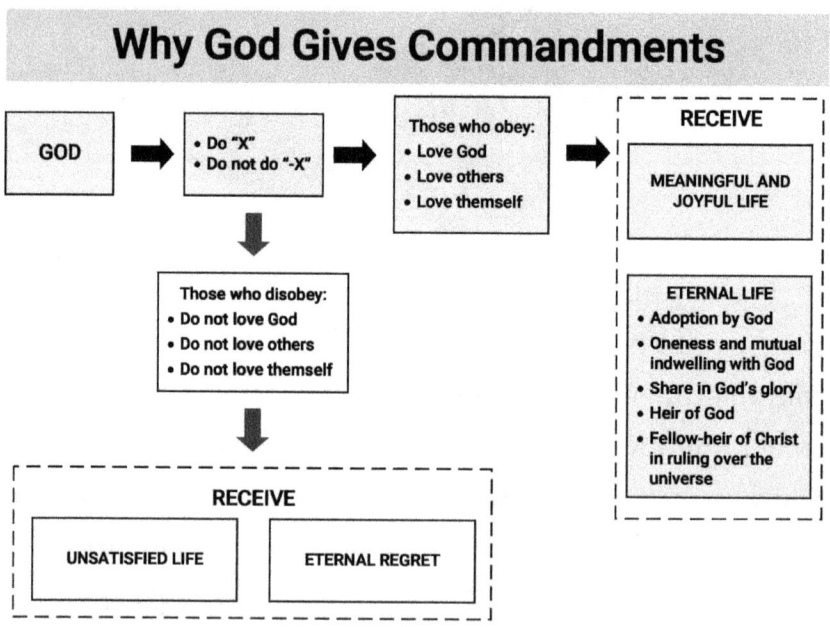

God gives commandments to help us become *compatible* with him so that we can have eternal glory as the Children of God who become his Son's fellow-heirs in ruling over the universe forever.

God does not care about what you know. He does not care about your wealth, fame, education, physical appearance, or how well you know the Bible. What he cares about, and cares enormously, is whether your attitude and behavior align with his commandments. Have you grown into someone who demonstrably loves God, loves others, and loves yourself?

- **Love God**: Do you strive to become someone who genuinely loves so that the God of love will joyfully share oneness and mutually-indwell with you? Do you do your best to obey him even when the world's morality opposes his will?

- **Love your neighbor**: Do you serve others by showing charity, kindness, and tolerance? Do you truly love your neighbor by being more concerned with their destiny as one of God's heirs and glorious rulers of the universe than in accepting and celebrating a lifestyle that violates God's words and commandments?

- **Love yourself**: Do you live according to eternal principles (such as by having integrity, eliminating harmful practices that make you loathe yourself, doing beneficial activities like diet and exercise, and continually improving)? Do you respect his temple—your body—by avoiding destructive addictions and violating his sexual rules?

Following God's commandments is not supposed to be easy, and the world will hate us for trying to obey him. But obedience is essential for a life of meaning now and eternal life in the next realm.

God never forces us to obey. He merely tells us what he expects and points out that those who follow the path he laid out will become his heirs and share in his oneness, nature, glory, and dominion. And since he makes the rules, not us, we can either obey and get the promise, or disobey and live forever with regret. And while we are certainly free to call his commandments "evil" and the world's latest moral fad "good," we will live forever with the consequences of our choices.

Excuses will not work when you stand before Christ to be judged. All your secrets and hidden desires will be exposed and taken into consideration. *Your actions and inactions determine your eternal fate.* If your neighbor loses their eternal life because you feared telling them to repent and obey God, then that is held against you. You will need to decide whether it is better to have your neighbor or God mad at you.

You must understand that *it does not matter what others do to you.* You do not need to inflict evil, hurt, and pain on someone just because you received evil, hurt, and pain.

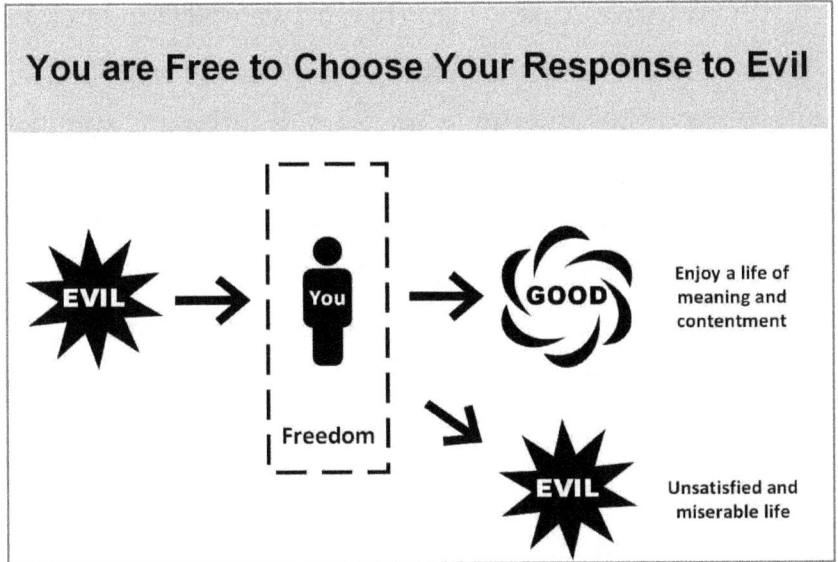

Follow Christ's example. This being of overwhelming glory and power as the almighty Creator of the universe and Earth *humbled* himself to become human. He *humbled* himself by washing the dirty feet of his followers. He *humbled* himself by absorbing all the pain and fear of collective humanity and dying without dignity on the cross. Note what he did not do: Although being God and the most powerful entity in the universe, he did not inflict evil when it was done to him.

The greatest of all became the least of all.

When we die, and we surely will, we will stand before him and see him in all his glory and majesty as our God[6] and inheritor of the universe. He will judge us, not just based on our works, but on what type of person we became while mortal. We can either dread the experience due to our filthiness or be filled with joy when he looks into our eyes because we used our brief time on earth to become a person of love, comparable to his nature as a God of love.

See *Is Jesus "God"? Chapter 10: Have a Meaningful Life* for more information.

The Biblical Jesus

If the Bible's core message is true, then Jesus also played the most vital parts in every aspect of our reality because he:

- Created the universe and keeps it together

---

[6] This book refers to Jesus as "our God" when emphasizing our relationship with him and describes him as "God" when considering his nature. He is "the Son of God" or distinct from "God" when contrasted with his Father. This does not make multiple "Gods" as they mutually indwell in each other, and all glory given to the Son is passed on to the Father.

- Saves humanity from the consequences of sin by suffering and dying for our sins – *if* we believe in him and *strive* to obey him

- Gives all humanity the gift of immortality by physically rising from the dead

- Helps us overcome our moral weaknesses and tolerate trials and hardship

- Receives the universe as his inheritance and shares it with his true followers

- Functions as the only way to God the Father and is his gatekeeper

- Replaces the earth with a new and better world

- Judges all humankind and gives eternal rewards/punishments

- Conjoins the God and human natures together so that *some* humans can share the divine nature he shares with the Father by "adoption" and become the "Children of God"

The Bible's message is a phenomenally powerful cosmology. One loses nothing important by believing in it and gains the infinite. <u>Even if it were *not* true</u>, belief in its message gives tangible benefits to a person, both internally and by positively influencing others and the world.

Jesus Christ's Atonement is the Most Important Event in the History of the Universe

If the Holy Bible's message about Jesus Christ is true, then he was the entity that created the universe.[7] He became human flesh two thousand years ago to conjoin the divine and human natures and perform an infinite atonement on our behalf.

Jesus Christ's infinite Atonement—our God's substitutionary suffering and death for our sakes—annulled the Fall (the introduction to humanity of death, sin, weakness, and trials). It was the ransom that freed us from captivity.

---

[7] John 1:3,10,14; Colossians 1:13-17; Hebrews 1:8-10; Hebrews 2:10 cf. 1 Corinthians 8:6; Hebrews 1:2-3; Revelation 3:14.

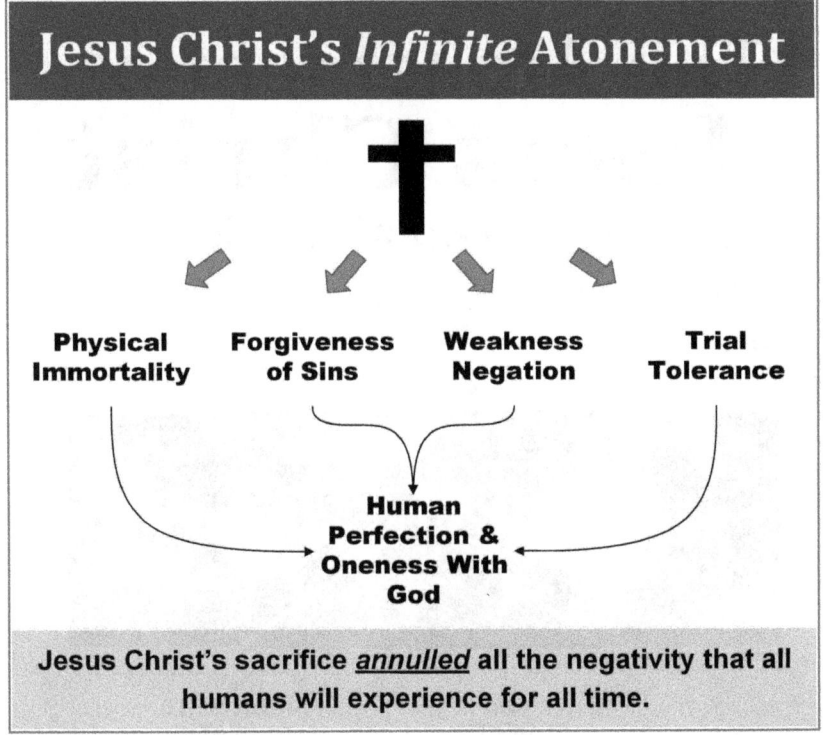

The Atonement was infinite – it applies to <u>all</u> humans for <u>all</u> time. There is no sin and negativity that humans will ever experience that it did not cover. It was also infinitely painful and infinitely terrifying. As the only sinless entity who is fully "God" and "Man," Jesus Christ was the only one who could perform it.

The Atonement of Jesus Christ
The *Pivot* Event of the Universe

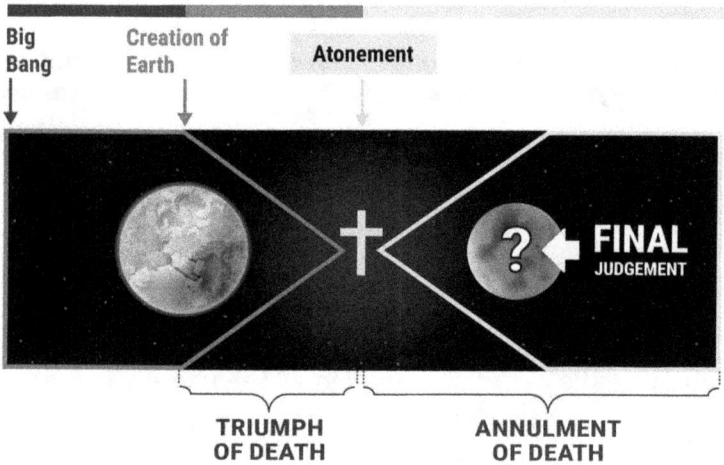

The Creator of the universe's suffering and death – the infinite Atonement – *annulled the Fall* (the introduction to humanity of death, sin, moral weakness, and trials) and changed the very nature of the cosmos.

The Atonement's conclusion, when Jesus resurrected, changed the very nature of the cosmos. Death used to dominate the universe; every living thing dies. But

Christ's successful Atonement means immortal life will now dominate the universe for all eternity.[8]

In other words, there will be physically immortal humans ruling over the universe beneath Christ's dominion who can never die (the "adopted" Children of God).

Christ's Atonement saves and perfects those who strive to follow him after conversion. It makes bad people good and good people better.

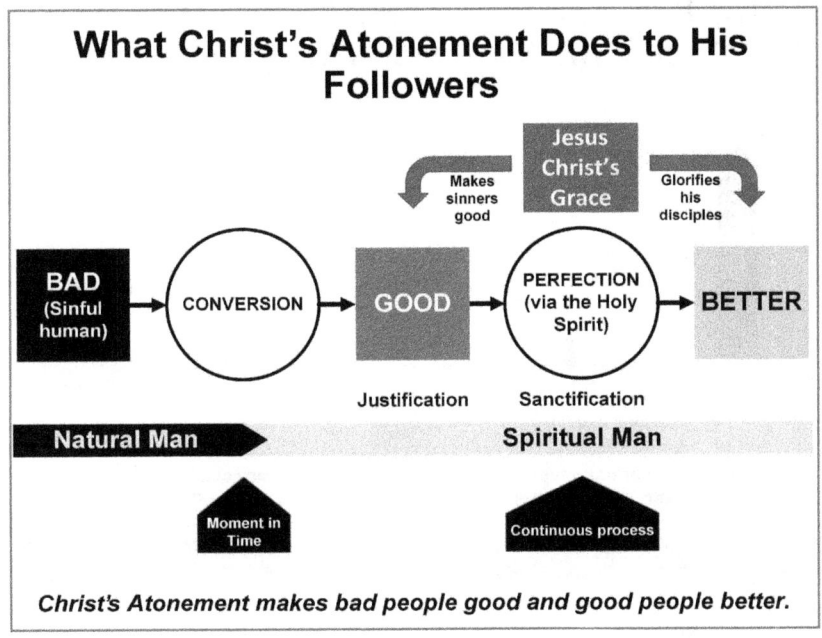

---

[8] Human life for sure, but, perhaps, also other immortal life forms. For instance, it is a nice idea to think that our pets experience immortality as well.

When the Christian receives the gift of the Holy Spirit after conversion and strives to follow Christ, the Holy Spirit uses the Savior's Atonement to perfect the person as they continuously have faith, repent, and walk the narrow path that leads to eternal life. The Christian can also pray to the Father to have Christ's Atonement help them overcome a moral weakness or tolerate a trial so that they continually become more "perfect" after conversion (to fulfill Christ's command in Matthew 5:48).

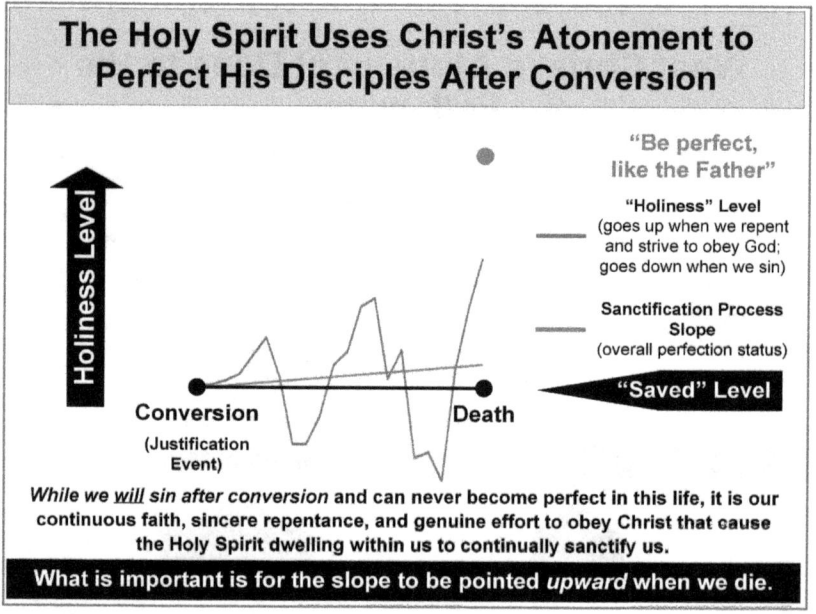

Of course, no one can obey perfectly; we need repentance every day. We must strive to be better, and regularly eat the body and drink the blood of Christ to become one with him and reset our sanctified state. When we do so, our sins are forgiven, and the Holy Spirit elevates us so that our moral slope points upward when we die, even when we backslide and collapse on occasion.

Christ's faithful disciples – those who prove themselves by their constant striving to follow him no matter what – are "adopted" by his Father[9] as the "Children of God" and become the Father's heirs and his Son's fellow-heirs over the universe.[10]

Christ's Atonement was infinite – infinite in that it covers all humans for all time and infinite in the sense of value, where an entity of infinite worth substituted himself for beings of finite worth. This infinite/finite substitution justifies the exaltation of those who become the Sons or Daughters of God by his grace, those who will reign with him over the universe for all eternity. No one can ever credibly contend that justice was cheated because all claims over us have been paid in full.

Christ's Atonement is the most important thing to have ever happened. It changed *everything*.

---

[9] Romans 8:15,22-23; Galatians 3:26-4:7; Ephesians 1:4-5.

[10] John 1:12-13; 1 John 2:29-3:3; 1 John 3:9; 1 John 5:1-5; Revelation 21:7; Romans 8:14-21; Galatians 3:26-4:7; Hebrews 2:10-17; Acts 20:32; Acts 26:18; Ephesians 1:11-18; Colossians 1:12-13; Colossians 3:24; Titus 3:7; Hebrews 1:14; Hebrews 9:15; James 2:5; 1 Peter 1:3-5.

How to Know That the Bible is Credible

Subjective Evidence: The Holy Spirit Tells You

Millions convert to the different branches of Christianity[11] every year because they feel the Holy Spirit within them as they read the Holy Bible. His presence gives them comfort, peace, joy, warmth, and a desire to do good and stop sinning. As they pray and ask God to teach them truth and reveal his will for them, the Holy Spirit testifies to the truthfulness of Jesus as God's Only Begotten Son and the only way to salvation.

This witness is subjective – no one can independently confirm in a lab that the Holy Spirit—that is, "God," communed with that person. But it is the most potent and convincing witness to the person. And the genuineness of

---

[11] Over 99.5% of all Christian denominations can be grouped into five branches containing multiple groups or families:

- Roman Catholic
- Eastern Christian
- Anglican/Independent Catholic
- Protestant
- Latter-day Saint

The five branches agree on the core biblical teachings for the most part but disagree on authority claims and interpretations.

the experience is seen by how the Christian changes their life to follow the pattern set by Jesus himself. To this day, thousands of Christians are killed every year for refusing to deny the Holy Spirit's witness.

This subjective witness caused Christians in the past half-millennium to change the world and usher in our technological civilization.

Objective Evidence: The New Testament is a Frameless, Unharmonized, Correlative Anthology

The New Testament is an astonishing triumph to those who understand the difficulties involved in creating correlative anthologies like textbooks or major project execution plans and request for proposal (RFP) responses.

Somehow, the New Testament, a collection of 27 books written by no less than nine people over a period of 50 years, has a single coherent cosmology. This is despite no single book or author describing the entire worldview. Each New Testament writer had pieces of a jigsaw puzzle or picture that could only be seen if all the pieces were put together.

42 | ODE TO JESUS

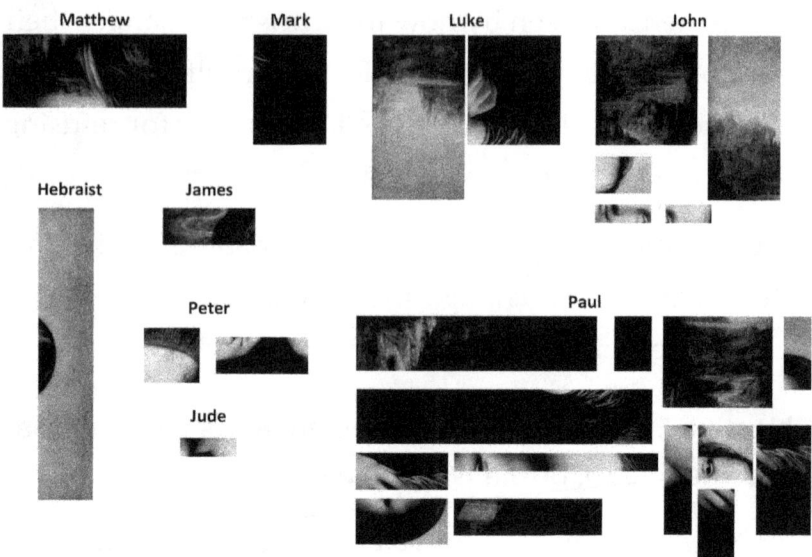

This does not happen with any other correlative anthology. A common frame such as specifications, standards, a style guide, author instructions, and team lead is always used by authors tasked to write different portions of a correlative anthology. In addition, a joint editor is always needed to harmonize deliverables from the different authors to create a unified message.

And yet, the New Testament did not have a common frame and common editor.

Somehow, the nine New Testament writers created a coherent picture comprised of abstract ideas without working within a common frame and without using a shared harmonizing editor.

This is empirically impossible.

How can the collective writings of the New Testament authors generate a single cosmology that so happens to have Jesus at the center of everything?

44 | ODE TO JESUS

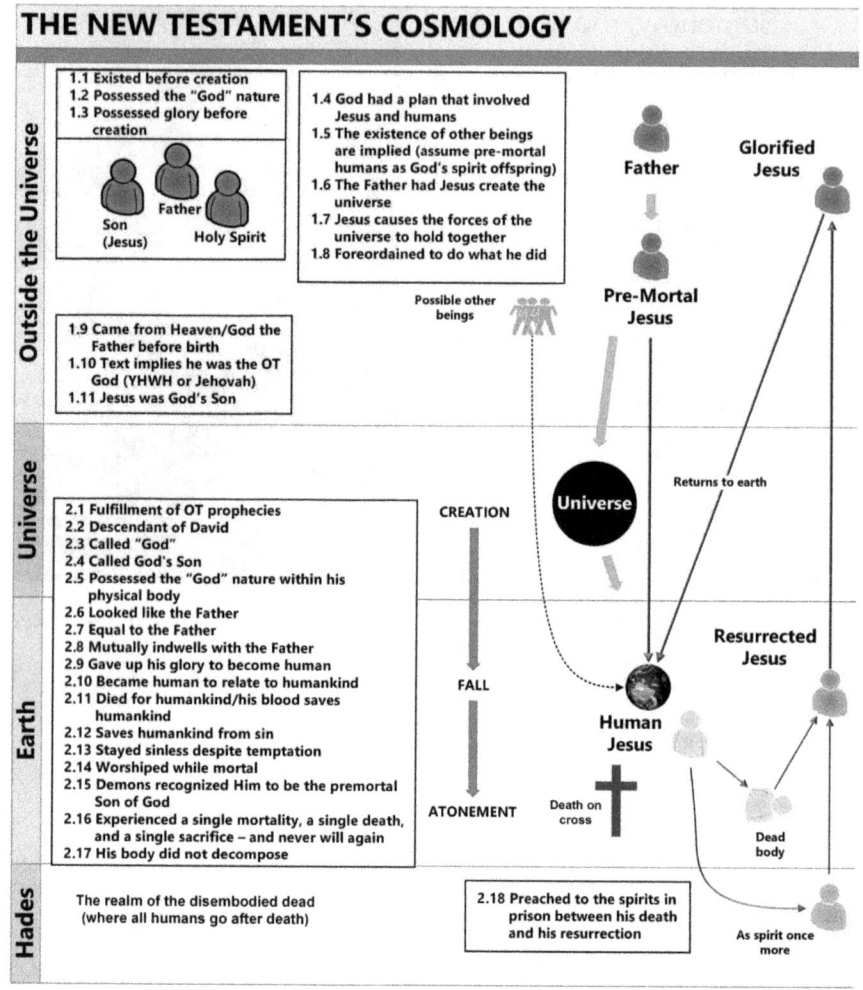

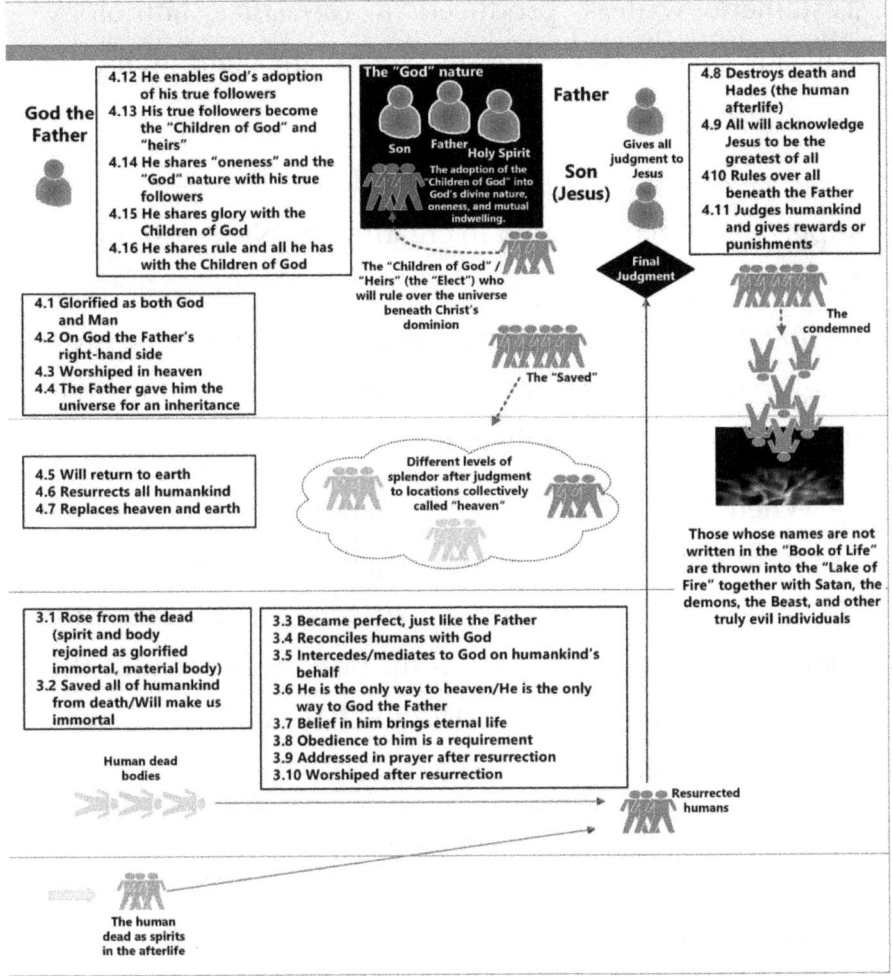

This coherent cosmology[12] should not exist – but it does! It is an impossibility since people cannot read each other's minds to produce harmonious deliverables of abstract ideas – but there it is! Somehow, the New

---

[12] See *Is Jesus "God"?* for the larger version and expansions on each subsection line item.

Testament writers produced a *correlative* anthology without using a common frame or employing a harmonizing editor.

It is a stunning piece of evidence that something supernatural participated in creating the New Testament. It challenges skeptics to explain how it is possible for nine people to magically combine their deliverables to create a single coherent picture or cosmology, given that it is demonstrably impossible to do so.[13]

When I saw the New Testament's cosmology, I instantly lost my atheism and regained my faith in Jesus Christ because I knew from experience that I was seeing something impossible. No group of writers without the leading common frame and lagging harmonizing edit can produce a coherent correlative anthology, especially one

---

[13] I have decades of experience as a technical writer and harmonizing technical editor for correlative anthologies such as project execution plans and RFP responses/proposals for very large projects. These documents use numerous authors whose deliverables need to blend to create a single voice or message. My job was to conduct a gap analysis, create content, and harmonize the deliverables before issuing the document. This makes me a subject matter expert on correlative anthologies.

of abstract ideas. I have been working in this area for most of my adult life; I do not doubt that it is real.

The significance of this discovery is profound:

Christians have had the objective evidence that Jesus is the Son of God all along in their hands!

It is as easy to demonstrate as tearing a sheet of paper into nine irregular sections and asking nine people to draw <u>parts</u> of something on their piece without telling them beforehand what to draw and without them knowing what the others intend to draw. After ten minutes, collect the pieces and see if they make a coherent image.

They will not. This is because multiple people cannot create perfectly harmonious pieces of a whole without operating within a common frame or using a common editor who will harmonize the deliverables to make a single whole. Some will write part of a house; others will write part of a tree, a face, or something else.

This is empirical and should give great comfort to every Christian and pause to those who dismiss Christianity. What this means is objective evidence exists that validates Christianity as the true religion. This is something no other religion has.

But while this aspect of the New Testament provides intellectual validation to the Christian's faith, it should never override the Holy Spirit's subjective witness since that communication from God is the most critical evidence one can receive to appreciate the Holy Bible and its message. It is more important than any miracle or even seeing an angel because one gets direct contact with God, resulting in an indelible stamp on their heart.

When the Holy Spirit reveals the truth about Jesus and his gospel to the person, that message overrides everything, and the Christian's faith becomes unshakeable. They then *know* Jesus is truly the Son of God and the only way we can be saved.

Strive to Become One of the Glorified and Exalted Children of God

Every one of us will die one day. It could be today, tomorrow, or in a hundred years – but we will surely die. We cannot avoid it, and its consequences are final. Death's unpredictability requires us to repent immediately and change for the better—leverage this fact to your advantage.

Now that you know that Jesus and the Holy Bible are credible, act; do not be content to be acted upon. Take charge of your life and control your destiny.

Christians of every denomination can take great comfort in knowing our faith in Jesus Christ has the testable evidence of the New Testament being a frameless, unharmonized, correlative anthology even though it does not need it. Christians can also be pleased to know that our faith has resulted in more tangible good to humanity than any other belief system—and everyone living today owes a great debt to it.

Christ's resurrection has sealed our fate and that of the universe. There is nothing anyone can do to impede his will and dominion over all of us and the entire cosmos. Everyone will eventually stand before him to be judged, and all will acknowledge Jesus is our Lord and God and deserves his glory and honor as the greatest of all.

A select few of us – those who strive to follow Christ wherever he leads us – will be exalted and transformed into the "Children of God." These glorious beings will dominate the universe as Christ's fellow-heirs and enjoy eternal oneness and mutual indwelling with the Father, Son, and Holy Spirit. These "elect" or "pre-destined" Children of God are characterized by the genuine love and charity in their hearts and their constant effort to do the best they can in obeying Christ, regardless of impediments and opposition.

No other religion has a concept of the afterlife that comes close to the ultimate fate of the New Testament's "Children of God." Their destiny is so enormous, so overwhelming, that our minds have difficulty comprehending God's magnificent promises:

- They will be "adopted" by God and share in the divine nature—the very essence of what makes God "God"
- They will enjoy oneness and mutual indwelling with God
- They will become God's heirs and fellow-heirs with Jesus
- They will share in God's glory
- They will share in Jesus Christ's rule and dominion over the universe (all things)

You have a choice; only you can decide what your eternity will look like. If you strive to follow Christ no matter what, then you can become one of the immortal rulers of the universe beneath Christ's dominion. Or you can use your *one* chance at mortality to become a slave to pride and the weaknesses of the flesh and live forever with regret.

Become Christ's true disciple in word and deed. Show love to God and others. Love yourself and keep the commandments. Repent every day and strive to be better. Forgive those who have wronged you. Be humble, and do not let your pride destroy your glorious future. Show genuine charity and compassion toward others – after all, Jesus Christ saves you because of his charity (you do not *deserve* to be saved).

You will know when you are on the right path by paying attention to the Holy Spirit dwelling within you and following his promptings. If you feel him leave or feel the joy that he gives disappear, you will immediately know that you have strayed and need to repent and go back to a state where he returns.

And when, not if, but when the world does not appreciate your contribution for good and tries to crush you or make you ashamed or afraid to be Jesus Christ's faithful follower: <u>Endure</u>. Ask Heavenly Father to have his Son's Atonement strengthen your resolve to obey and stay faithful.

While our mortal life is just a "blink-of-an-eye" of our overall existence, our choices here dictate what we become in the eternities to come. Choose wisely.

My Witness

I know Jesus is God's Only Begotten Son who died for our sins and is the only way we can be saved. Jesus is *my* God, just as the Father is my God.

There was a time when I rejected him and lived as an atheist for many years. While writing what became *Is Jesus "God"?* in early 2016 and seeing the New Testament's core message fall into place, my faith suddenly reappeared because I know firsthand that different people cannot have the same perspective about anything, especially if not sharing a common frame to put constraints on their views, and not using a common editor to harmonize their perspectives.

This single coherent cosmology means the New Testament contains empirical evidence of God within itself. But we have never noticed it before because we are so used to assuming the New Testament is a single book instead of an anthology or collection of books.

I am a flawed man. I am a sinner. I am weak. But in Christ, I can become perfect. Through him, my sins are washed away. And he makes me strong.

Again, come with me and raise your voice to heaven. Let us sing together. Praise our Lord and Savior. Praise our God who took upon himself our sins and paid our ransom!

PART 2: ODE TO JESUS HYMNS

Prologue

Meter 87.87

---

(1) There are many things we do not know.
Seekers seek explanation.
Four big questions without answer.
All to do with creation.

(2) How did the cosmos come to be?
Fine-tuned for life's emergence!
What or who caused the universe?
Science and faith's convergence!

(3) How did living things come to be?
Living cell's complexity!
How did complex come from simple?
Impossible chemistry!

(4) How did modern man come to be?
With stunning ability!
What's with our superiority?
Reason and morality?

(5) The New Testament has one voice.
It shouldn't have, but it has!
Many authors, but one message.
Removed by time and distance!
No common editor nor frame.
Correlative components!
Impossible accomplishment.
Great joy to its proponents!

(6) The world owes a great debt to Christ.
Mankind's life is much better!
Tangible benefits to all –
All thanks to his followers!
Foundation of all our science.
Annulment of slavery!
Innate value of all humans.
Real freedom from tyranny!

(7) *So, come, and meet the real Jesus –*
The one who improved your life!
Discover who he truly is.
Why not have eternal life?

1. The Pre-Existence of Jesus

Meter 86.86

(a)   In the beginning was the Word.
And the Word was with God!
He existed before the world.
And ere the universe!

(b)   The Son has the Father's nature.
By nature, he is God!
The Son radiates God's glory.
Exact image of God!

(c)   He had glory ere creation.
He shared God's glory!
He gave up his equality.
He emptied his glory!

(d)   He was foreordained to atone –
Before the world was made!
He was ordained to save mankind,
Before the earth was laid!

THE PRE-EXISTENCE OF JESUS | 57

(e) He came from heaven before birth.
The Son came from heaven!
He gave up heaven to come here.
God's only Son left heaven!

(f) Jesus came from God the Father.
Thank you, God, for your Son!
Jesus was sent by his Father.
Thank you, O Holy One!

(g) Jesus is the Lord of Israel.
He is the Great I AM!
God's only Son is the Lord of lords.
He is the King of kings!

(h) God gave his only Son for us.
His great work had begun!
God's Son obeyed his Father's will.
Thank you, Lord, for your Son!

STANZA REFERENCES

(a) **HE EXISTED BEFORE CREATION**: John 1:1-3,10,14; 1 John 1:1-2; 1 John 2:13; Colossians 1:15-17; 1 Peter 1:19-20; 2 Timothy 1:9-10

- (b) **HE WAS "GOD" BY NATURE:** John 1:1; Philippians 2:5-7; Hebrews 1:2-3

- (c) **HE POSSESSED GLORY:** John 17:5,22,24; Philippians 2:6-8

- (d) **HE WAS FOREORDAINED TO BE THE SINLESS SUBSTITUTE:** Acts 3:20; 1 Peter 1:20

- (e) **HE CAME FROM HEAVEN:** John 3:13,31-32; John 6:33,38,41-42,50-51,58,62; John 8:23; 1 Corinthians 15:47; Ephesians 4:9-10

- (f) **HE CAME FROM THE FATHER:** John 3:16-17; John 6:32,38-40,44,46,57; John 7:33-34; John 8:18,42; John 10:36; John 12:41-50; John 13:3; John 16:5; John 16:28; John 17:3,8,21,23,25; 1 John 4:9-10,14; Romans 8:3; Galatians 4:4

- (g) **HE WAS THE OLD TESTAMENT GOD:** (John 8:24,28,58; John 13:19; John 18:5-8 cf. Exodus 3:14; Deuteronomy 32:39; Isaiah 41:4; Isaiah 43:10; Isaiah 46:4) / (Acts 4:10-12; 1 John 4:14 cf. Isaiah 43:11; Hosea 13:4); Revelation 17:14; Revelation 19:13-16

- (h) **HE IS GOD'S ONLY BEGOTTEN SON:** Matthew 3:17; Matthew 17:5; Hebrews 1:5; 2 Peter 1:17; John 1:14; John 3:16,18,35; 1 John 4:9-10

2. Jesus Mutually Indwells With the Father

Meter 86.86

(a)   Father, Son, and Holy Spirit–
They dwell in each other!
Whether by will or innately,
Within one another!

(b)   Christ is in the image of God.
God's glory on his face!
He is an exact duplicate –
Of God's very essence!

(c)   The Son is in God the Father.
The Father's in the Son!
They indwell in one another.
Always within each one!

(d)   The Son is one with the Father.
Father and Son are one!
Jesus said God was one with him.
A oneness with the Son!

JESUS MUTUALLY INDWELLS WITH THE FATHER

(e) The Father glorifies the Son.
Christ gives glory to God!
God honors Christ within himself.
Son's glorified by God!

(f) The Son's equal to the Father.
Eternal equality!
Equal praise to Father and Son.
Equal eternally!

(g) God's fulness dwelt in Christ's body.
God's fulness in his flesh!
God's fulness was in his body.
God's fulness in Christ's flesh!

(h) To see one, one sees the other.
Jesus, show me your face!
To see him, one sees the Father.
Father, give us your grace!

STANZA REFERENCES

(a) **THE FATHER, SON, AND HOLY SPIRIT SHARE A COMMON SPACE**: John 10:38; John 14:10-11,20; John 17:21,23; 2 Corinthians 5:19

- **(b)** **HE IS IN THE IMAGE OF GOD**: 2 Corinthians 4:4-6; Colossians 1:15; Hebrews 1:2-3

- **(c)** **HE IS IN THE FATHER; THE FATHER IS IN HIM**: John 10:38; John 14:10-11,20; John 17:21,23; John 13:31-32; 2 Corinthians 5:19

- **(d)** **HE IS ONE WITH THE FATHER**: John 10:30; John 17:11,21-22

- **(e)** **THE FATHER IS GLORIFIED IN JESUS**: John 13:31-32; 2 Corinthians 5:19

- **(f)** **HE IS EQUAL TO THE FATHER**: John 5:17-18; John 10:33; John 5:23; John 14:16; John 16:26; John 17:9,15,20

- **(g)** **THE FULNESS OF GOD WAS WITHIN HIS BODY**: Colossians 1:19; Colossians 2:9

- **(h)** **ONE SEES THE FATHER WHEN LOOKING AT JESUS**: John 12:45; John 14:7-12

JESUS MUTUALLY INDWELLS WITH THE FATHER | 63

3. Jesus is the Almighty Creator

Meter 86.86

(a) God made the universe through Christ.
Sire ordered; Son obeyed!
This reality came to be –
Father designed; Son made!

(b) God's only Son made the cosmos.
Every planet and star!
He made the big bang's time and space.
And all things near and far!

(c) Nothing exists without Christ's word.
There's naught he didn't make!
Everything in heaven and earth –
All things he did create!

(d) Jesus sustains the universe.
He keeps it together!
By the power of our Lord's word –
He holds it together!

(e) The Son of God formed this great world.
He created this earth!
Although man did not know he did.
Made long before his birth!

(f) He breathed life into matter.
Structured life formed from clay!
He brought complexity from base.
In all of life's array!

(g) Most of all, he created man.
The pinnacle of life!
Capable of moral reason.
Can discern wrong from right!

(h) He gave us genuine freedom.
We are free to obey him!
He does not force us to be good.
We must freely heed him!

STANZA REFERENCES

(a) **THE FATHER CREATED THE UNIVERSE THROUGH HIM**: 1 Corinthians 8:6; Hebrews 1:2-3; Revelation 3:14

- (b) **HE CREATED THE UNIVERSE:** John 1:3,10,14; Colossians 1:13-17; Hebrews 1:8-10; Hebrews 2:10

- (c) **NOTHING EXISTS THAT WAS NOT CREATED BY HIM:** John 1:3; Colossians 1:13-17

- (d) **HE SUSTAINS THE UNIVERSE:** Colossians 1:17; Hebrews 1:3

- (e) **HE CREATED THIS EARTH:** John 1:10; Colossians 1:16; Hebrews 1:8-10

- (f) **HE CREATED LIFE:** Colossians 1:16

- (g) **HE CREATED MAN:** 1 Corinthians 8:6; Colossians 1:16

- (h) **WE HAVE FREE WILL:** Mark 8:34; John 1:12-13; Romans 10:9-10; 2 Corinthians 9:7; Galatians 5:1,13; Revelation 3:20

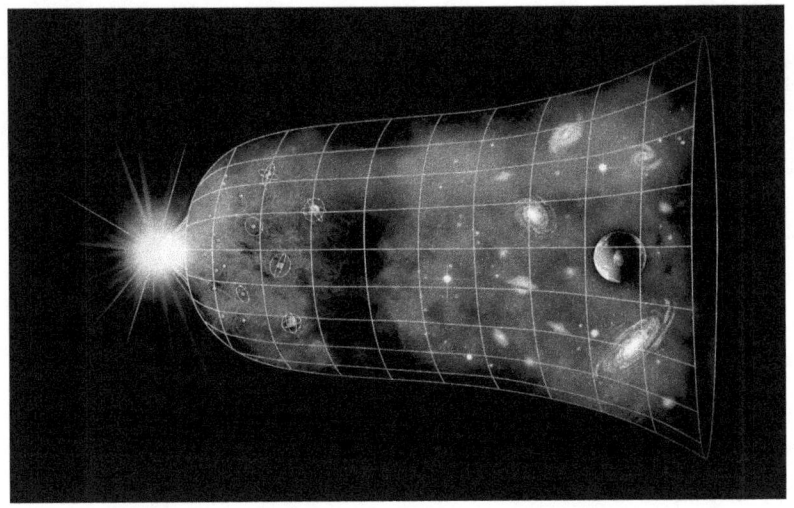

4. Jesus Became Human

Meter 86.86

(a)   The Creator became human.
Jesus Christ became flesh!
By becoming a mortal man.
He dignified our flesh!

(b)   He transformed from spirit to flesh.
He changed his state to mine!
Without this metamorphosis,
He couldn't save mankind!

(c)   He needed to relate to man.
He had to become man!
Jesus condemned sin in the flesh.
By becoming human!

(d)   Jesus bridged divine and human.
He was both God and man!
He was not half-God and half-man –
He was full God and man!

(e) He humbled himself to be born.
The great God became man!
He emptied himself of glory.
From divine to mere man!

(f) He was tempted but never sinned.
Jesus never sinned!
He resisted all temptation.
Our Lord stayed free from sin!

(g) He only becomes mortal once.
Just one mortality!
Death cannot again embrace him.
He rules death and Hades!

(h) The devils recognized Jesus.
They knew he was God's Son!
They begged him to let them be.
They feared God's only Son!

STANZA REFERENCES

(a) **HE BECAME FLESH**: John 1:14; 1 John 4:2-3; 2 John 1:7; Romans 8:3

(b) **HE BECAME FLESH TO BECOME A REAL HUMAN**: John 1:14; 1 John 4:2-3; 2 John 1:7; Romans 8:3; Hebrews 2:14-17

(c) **HE BECAME HUMAN TO RELATE TO HUMANITY**: John 3:16; 1 John 1:1-2; Romans 1:3; 1 Corinthians 15:21; Galatians 4:4; Philippians 2:7-8; Hebrews 2:14-18; Revelation 5:5,9,12

(d) **HE BRIDGED THE GOD AND HUMAN NATURES**: John 1:1; Hebrews 1:2-3 cf. John 3:16; 1 John 1:1-2; Romans 1:3; 1 Corinthians 15:21; Galatians 4:4; Philippians 2:7-8; Hebrews 2:14-18; Colossians 1:20-22; Revelation 5:5,9,12

(e) **HE HUMBLED HIMSELF TO BECOME HUMAN**: Philippians 2:7-8

(f) **HE WAS TEMPTED BUT NEVER SINNED**: 2 Corinthians 5:21; Hebrews 4:15; Hebrews 7:26; Hebrews 9:14; 1 Peter 2:22; 1 John 3:5; Hebrews 2:18; Matthew 4:1,7

(g) **HE CAN ONLY HAVE A SINGLE INCARNATION**: Romans 6:9-10; Romans 8:34; 2 Corinthians 5:15; John 10:15; Romans 6:10; Hebrews 7:27; Hebrews 9:12,25-28; Hebrews 10:10-14; 1 Peter 3:18

JESUS BECAME HUMAN | 71

(h) **HE WAS RECOGNIZED BY DEMONS:** Mark 1:34;
Mark 3:11-12; Luke 4:41

5. The Atonement of Jesus

Meter 86.86

(a) Jesus suffered for mankind's sins.
He took our punishments!
God placed upon himself our sins,
To save us from torments!

(b) Christ's Atonement was infinite.
Pain, inconceivable!
It was infinite hurt and fear.
Unimaginable!

(c) He was a sinless substitute.
He was the Lamb of God!
He was a stain-free sacrifice.
An offering to God!

(d) Jesus ransomed himself for us.
Because of him, we're free!
Christ's holy blood paid the ransom.
We slaves can now be free!

THE ATONEMENT OF JESUS | 73

(e)   Jesus died for humanity.
He died for you and me!
God's only Son died for our sins.
Despite we're not worthy!

(f)   He reconciles us to our God.
His blood justifies us!
His sacrifice reconciles us.
His blood sanctifies us!

(g)   We're redeemed through his holy blood.
We're washed clean in his blood!
His shed blood removes mankind's sins.
Made sinless through his blood!

(h)   We are nailed to the cross with him.
We're crucified with Christ!
We share his death; we share his rise.
We live to God in Christ!

STANZA REFERENCES

(a)   **HE SUFFERED**: Matthew 20:28; Romans 3:23-25; Romans 8:32; Galatians 1:4; 1 Timothy 2:6; Titus 2:14; Hebrews 10:10-20; 1 Peter 1:11,18-20; 1 Peter 2:21-24; 1 John 4:9-10,14; Luke 22:42-44; Acts 26:23; Hebrews 5:7-9

- **(b)** **HE EXPERIENCED AN INFINITE ATONEMENT**: 1 Timothy 2:6; Hebrews 10:10-20; 1 Peter 1:11,18-20; Hebrews 2:9-10; Colossians 1:20-22; Hebrews 7:25-28; Hebrews 9:11-28; 1 Peter 3:18; Revelation 5:9

- **(c)** **HE WAS A SINLESS SUBSTITUTE**: Matthew 20:28; Romans 3:23-25; Romans 8:32; Galatians 1:4; 1 Timothy 2:6; Titus 2:14; Hebrews 10:10-20; 1 Peter 1:11,18-20; 1 Peter 2:21-24; 1 John 4:9-10,14

- **(d)** **HE PAID OUR RANSOM AND FREED US**: Galatians 1:4; Galatians 3:13; 1 Timothy 2:6; Titus 2:14; 1 Peter 1:18-20; Revelation 1:5

- **(e)** **HE DIED FOR HUMANKIND**: John 10:15,17-18; John 17:19; Romans 5:6-8; 2 Corinthians 5:14-15; Galatians 2:20-21; 1 Thessalonians 5:9-10; Hebrews 2:9-10; Hebrews 9:15,26-28

- **(f)** **HIS SACRIFICE/BLOOD RECONCILES US TO GOD**: Romans 5:9-11; Ephesians 2:13-16; Colossians 1:20-22; Hebrews 7:25-28; Hebrews 9:11-28; 1 Peter 3:18; Revelation 1:5; Revelation 5:9

- **(g)** **HIS BLOOD FORGIVES SINS**: Matthew 26:28; Luke 22:15-16,19-20,42-44; Ephesians 1:7; Hebrews 9:11-14; 1 John 1:7

- **(h)** **WE PARTICIPATE WITH HIM**: Romans 6:3-11; Romans 7:4; Romans 8:17; 2 Corinthians 4:14; Galatians 2:20-21; Ephesians 2:5-6; Philippians 3:10; Colossians 2:14; 2 Timothy 2:11; 1 Peter 2:24

6. The Resurrection of Jesus

Meter 86.86

(a)   Meeting the spirits in prison,
Jesus preached to the dead!
The Son of God fulfilled his task –
His suffering ended!

(b)   Angels proclaimed glorious news:
Jesus came back from death!
He is not here; he is risen.
He once again has breath!

(c)   Jesus Christ was resurrected.
Jesus conquered the grave!
Returning from the realm of death,
Never again death's slave!

(d)   He spent time with his disciples.
His body could be felt!
Forty days they walked together,
Then rising up to dwelt!

(e)   He's first to be resurrected.

The first immortal flesh!

Our Lord's the firstborn from the dead.

Praise him who conquered death!

(f)   Christ will forever destroy death.

I no longer fear death!

Christ holds the keys of death and Hades.

Jesus will annul death!

(g)   Jesus can never die again.

Just one mortality!

Death can never again have him.

He lives eternally!

(h)   Christ makes everyone immortal –

Both righteous and flawed!

This bequest he gives to us all.

In our flesh, we'll see God!

STANZA REFERENCES

(a) **HE PREACHED TO THE SPIRITS IN PRISON**: 1 Peter 3:18-20

(b) **ANGELS ANNOUNCED HIS RESURRECTION**: Matthew 28:5-7; Luke 24:3-8

(c) **HE ROSE FROM THE DEAD**: Mark 16:9; Acts 13:37; Acts 17:31; Romans 6:9-10; 1 Corinthians 15:4,12-26; 2 Corinthians 5:15; Ephesians 1:20; 1 Thessalonians 4:14; 2 Timothy 2:8; 1 Peter 3:21

(d) **MANY EYEWITNESSES SAW, INTERACTED WITH, AND FELT THE RESURRECTED JESUS**: Matthew 28:9; Luke 24:36-51; Acts 1:1-11; John 20:19-20; John 20:25-29; 1 Corinthians 15:5-8

(e) **HE WAS FIRST TO RESURRECT FROM THE DEAD WITH AN IMMORTAL BODY**: Acts 26:23; 1 Corinthians 15:20,23; Colossians 1:18; Revelation 1:5

(f) **HE WILL DESTROY DEATH AND HADES**: 1 Corinthians 15:26; 2 Timothy 1:10; Revelation 20:13-14; Revelation 1:18

(g) **HE CAN NEVER DIE AGAIN**: Romans 6:9-10; Romans 8:34; 2 Corinthians 5:15

(h) **HE MAKES EVERYONE IMMORTAL**: Acts 24:15; John 5:28-29; Romans 5:15-18; 1 Corinthians 15:12-30; 1 Corinthians 15:35,40-57

THE RESURRECTION OF JESUS

7. The Glorification of Jesus

Meter 86.86

(a) The Father glorifies his Son.
He has God's own glory!
Christ is exalted above all.
Because he was worthy!

(b) His name is above all names.
Jesus is over all!
All will concede Jesus is Lord.
Jesus is Lord of all!

(c) Exalted to the Father's right.
Our Lord's at God's right hand!
Seat of honor, might, and glory –
Before of which we'll stand!

(d) Jesus is the only way to God.
He stands before God's throne!
No one can receive salvation –
Lest going through God's Son!

THE GLORIFICATION OF JESUS | 81

(e)   God gave his Son the universe.
Dominion over all!
An eternal inheritance.
Beneath his feet are all!

(f)   Jesus Christ will return to earth.
He will come suddenly!
With angels and the righteous dead.
With great might and glory!

(g)   Jesus will resurrect us all;
Both the good and the bad!
He will judge all men and women –
To be saved or condemned!

(h)   He will replace heaven and earth.
A new heaven and earth!
The old versions obsoleted;
The new: No sin, no death!

STANZA REFERENCES

(a)   **HE IS GLORIFIED AND EXALTED ABOVE ALL**: Acts 2:32-33; John 13:31-32; John 17:1-2,5,24; Revelation 5:5,9,12-13; Hebrews 2:9; Hebrews 7:26; 2 Peter 1:17; Philippians 2:9-11; 1 Peter 3:22; Ephesians 1:21

(b) **HIS NAME IS ABOVE ALL NAMES/HE IS LORD**: Philippians 2:9-11; Revelation 5:13-14

(c) **HE IS EXALTED TO GOD'S RIGHT-HAND SIDE**: Matthew 26:64; Mark 14:62; Mark 16:19; Luke 22:69; Acts 2:32-33; Acts 7:55-56; Romans 8:34; Ephesians 1:20; Colossians 3:1; Hebrews 1:13; Hebrews 8:1; Hebrews 10:12; Hebrews 12:2; 1 Peter 3:22

(d) **HE IS THE ONLY WAY TO GOD/HE IS THE ONLY WAY FOR US TO BE SAVED**: John 14:6; Revelation 7:17; 1 Timothy 2:5; Acts 4:10-12

(e) **HE IS GIVEN THE UNIVERSE AS AN INHERITANCE AND REIGNS OVER IT**: Matthew 11:27; John 3:35; Hebrews 1:2; Hebrews 2:10; Matthew 28:18; John 13:3; Romans 9:5; Colossians 1:16-20; John 16:15; John 17:10; Matthew 19:28; Acts 10:36; 1 Corinthians 15:25-28; Ephesians 1:10,20-23

(f) **HE WILL RETURN TO EARTH WITH GREAT POWER AND GLORY**: Matthew 26:64; Colossians 3:4; 1 Thessalonians 5:9-10; 2 Thessalonians 1:7-10; 2 Thessalonians 2:8; 1 Timothy 6:14; 2 Timothy 4:1,8; Titus 2:13; Hebrews 9:28; 1 Peter 5:4; Revelation 22:12; Luke 12:40; Matt 16:27; Matt 25:31; 1 Corinthians 15:23; 1 Thessalonians 3:13; 1 Thessalonians 4:14-17; Jude 1:14; Mark 14:62; Matthew 24:30; Acts 1:9-11

THE GLORIFICATION OF JESUS | 83

(g) **HE WILL RESURRECT AND JUDGE HUMANKIND:** Revelation 1:18; Acts 24:15; 1 Corinthians 15:12-30; Matthew 16:27; Matthew 25:31-34,41,46; John 5:22-30; Revelation 20:10-15; Revelation 22:12; Acts 10:42; Acts 17:31; 2 Corinthians 5:10; 2 Timothy 4:1; 1 Peter 4:5-6

(h) **HE WILL REPLACE HEAVEN AND EARTH:** Matthew 19:28; Hebrews 1:10-12; 2 Peter 3:10-13; Revelation 21:1,5; Revelation 20:11; Romans 8:19-21

8. Jesus Creates the Children of God

Meter 86.86

(a)   Follow Christ for eternal life.
Believe him and be saved!
He's the living bread from heaven.
Have faith, repent, be kind!

(b)   We are to keep his commandments.
Believe him and obey!
Do good and show love and mercy.
Love all, and always pray!

(c)   God adopts us because of Christ.
We can be born of God!
The Lord's foster sons and daughters.
By grace, Children of God!

(d)   The Children of God are his heirs.
By grace, we are his heirs!
No longer specks, but now his heirs.
With Jesus, fellow-heirs!

(e)   God's children share oneness with him.
Dwelling in each other!
We live in them; they live in us.
None without the other!

(f)   Sharing in the divine nature,
God shares himself with us!
Transforming to Christ's same image,
Awaits his followers!

(g)   Christ shares glory with God's children.
God's heirs share in glory!
Christ gives us his glory from God.
His heirs receive glory!

(h)   Jesus shares all he has with us –
For those who stay faithful!
Those who endure will rule with him –
A gift so wonderful!

STANZA REFERENCES

(a) **BELIEF IN HIM BRINGS SALVATION**: Matthew 19:27-29; John 3:15-16,36; John 6:40,47,51,54-58; John 10:28; John 17:2-3; 1 John 1:2; 1 John 2:25; 1 John 5:9-13,20; Romans 5:21; Romans 6:23; Titus 3:7; Hebrews 5:9; 1 Peter 5:10; Jude 1:21

(b) **WE MUST OBEY HIM**: Romans 1:5; Romans 6:16; Romans 16:26; Hebrews 5:9; 1 Peter 1:2; 1 Peter 1:13-14,22-23; John 15:10; 1 John 5:3; 2 John 1:4,6

(c) **HE ENABLES HIS FOLLOWERS TO BE ADOPTED BY GOD**: Romans 8:15,22-23; Galatians 3:26-4:7; Ephesians 1:4-5

(d) **HIS TRUE FOLLOWERS BECOME THE CHILDREN OF GOD AND GOD'S HEIRS**: John 1:12-13; 1 John 2:29-3:3; 1 John 3:9; 1 John 5:1-5; Revelation 21:7; Romans 8:14-21; Galatians 3:26-4:7; Hebrews 2:10-17; Acts 20:32; Acts 26:18; Ephesians 1:11-18; Colossians 1:12-13; Colossians 3:24; Titus 3:7; Hebrews 1:14; Hebrews 9:15; James 2:5; 1 Peter 1:3-5

(e) **THE CHILDREN OF GOD SHARE ONENESS AND MUTUAL INDWELLING WITH GOD**: John 15:1-11; John 17:11,21-23; Romans 8:16-17; 1 Corinthians 6:17; Galatians 3:26-29; John 6:56; John 14:20,23; 1 John 5:20; Romans 8:9-11; 1 Corinthians 3:16-17; Galatians 2:20; Ephesians 1:4; Colossians 1:27

JESUS CREATES THE CHILDREN OF GOD

(f) THE CHILDREN OF GOD SHARE THE DIVINE NATURE: Romans 8:28-30; 1 Corinthians 1:9; 1 Corinthians 15:48-49; 2 Corinthians 3:18; 2 Corinthians 8:9; Ephesians 3:19; Ephesians 4:13,15,24; Colossians 2:9-10; Colossians 3:10; Hebrews 3:14; Hebrews 12:9-10; 2 Peter 1:3-4; 1 John 1:3-7; 1 John 2:29-3:3

(g) THE CHILDREN OF GOD SHARE GLORY: John 17:22; Romans 5:2; Colossians 3:4; 2 Timothy 2:10; 2 Peter 1:3-4; Romans 8:17-21,28-30; Romans 9:23-24; 2 Corinthians 4:17; Ephesians 1:11-18; Colossians 1:27; 1 Thessalonians 2:12; 2 Thessalonians 2:13-14; Hebrews 2:10

(h) THE CHILDREN OF GOD SHARE RULE AND EVERYTHING HE HAS: Revelation 3:21; Revelation 20:4; 2 Timothy 2:12; Luke 12:44; Romans 8:32; 1 Corinthians 3:21-23; 2 Corinthians 6:10; Hebrews 3:14; 2 Timothy 4:7-8; James 1:12; Luke 12:32; Luke 22:29-30; Ephesians 2:5-7; James 2:5; Revelation 1:6; Revelation 5:10; Revelation 22:5; Revelation 21:7; Mark 13:13

Epilogue

Meter 86.86

---

(1)   Jesus was, before time and space.
With the Father was he!
Before the universe became,
The Son of God was he!

(2)   Father, Son, and Holy Spirit –
They dwell in each other!
To see the Son, one sees his sire.
The Son's like the Father!

(3)   He made the universe and earth –
Billions of years ago!
He made life from sterile matter.
He formed us long ago!

(4)   Jesus Christ humbly became man.
He became human flesh!
Abandoning his great glory,
God conjoined with our flesh!

(5)   He placed upon himself our sins.
He took our hurt and sins!
An infinite substitution –
For those who accept him!

(6)   Christ died in ghastly pain and fear.
The Lord disrespected!
And yet our Lord came back to life.
Jesus resurrected!

(7)   He triumphed over sin and death.
His name's above all names!
He will judge all men and women.
To eternal acclaims!

(8)   Jesus calls us to follow him.
He saves those who obey!
He makes us the Children of God.
Please, Lord, show us the way!

PART 3: HYMN STANZA CLARIFICATIONS

Part 3 conducts a "deep dive" into each hymn's stanza. You will see at least one scriptural passage validating the concept detailed in the core hymn's stanza. This proves that the idea is clearly found in the Holy Bible.

What this portion of the book does *not* do is quote *all* the biblical passages identified below each Part 2 hymn. You are encouraged to do some work on your own by using your personal Bible or an online resource like Bible Hub or Bible Gateway to confirm the validity of the cited passages below each hymn.

There is a reason for this: **Act; do not be content to be acted upon.** You will obtain greater value and appreciation of the Holy Bible's actual teachings by putting in the effort to learn on your own instead of from me giving you all the answers. But at least now, your study is much more effective because Part 2 identifies where to look to find validation.

Methodology

Each Part 2 hymn stanza has at least one paraphrased scripture quotation based on Nestle-Aland 28, which many biblical scholars consider to be the most accurate New Testament of modern times.

These conceptual (not linguistic) paraphrases are taken from *IS JESUS "GOD"?* where the following methodology was done to each NT verse that resulted in a paraphrased output:

Colossians 1:16-17

Colossians 1:16	
https://www.biblegateway.com/verse/en/col%201:16	

Nestle-Aland 28	ὅτι ἐν αὐτῷ ἐκτίσθη τὰ πάντα ἐν τοῖς οὐρανοῖς καὶ ἐπὶ τῆς γῆς, τὰ ὁρατὰ καὶ τὰ ἀόρατα, εἴτε θρόνοι εἴτε κυριότητες εἴτε ἀρχαὶ εἴτε ἐξουσίαι·τὰ πάντα δι' αὐτοῦ καὶ εἰς αὐτὸν ἔκτισται·
Transliteration	hoti en autō ektisthē ta panta en tois ouranois kai epi tēs gēs, ta horata kai ta aorata, eite thronoi eite kyriotētes eite archai eite exousiai; ta panta di' autou kai eis auton ektistai;
Paraphrase	*He created the universe. Everything in heaven and earth, everything we see and cannot see, including thrones, powers, rulers, or authorities; he created them all, and they are for him.*

Colossians 1:17	
https://www.biblegateway.com/verse/en/col%201:17	
Nestle-Aland 28	καὶ αὐτός ἐστιν πρὸ πάντων καὶ τὰ πάντα ἐν αὐτῷ συνέστηκεν,
Transliteration	kai autos estin pro pantōn kai ta panta en autō synestēken,
Paraphrase	*He existed before the universe and causes it to hold together.*

Col 1:16-17 He created the universe. Everything in heaven and earth, everything we see and cannot see, including thrones, powers, rulers, or authorities; he created them all, and they are for him. 17 He existed before the universe and causes it to hold together.

Each examined verse in *IS JESUS "GOD"?* has a link and QR code that leads the reader to Bible Gateway's over 50 parallel bibles to demonstrate that the paraphrases align with most bibles today. In addition, transliterations are provided to help those who want to pronounce the Greek text and ease learning the biblical language.

The Prologue hymn does not contain any scripture references since it is focused on science and logic. Neither is a similar methodology done to the Epilogue hymn since it merely summarizes each of the core eight hymns into a corresponding stanza of its own.

Let us now dive into each of the Part 2 hymn stanzas.

Clarification of the "Prologue" Stanzas

Stanza 1

> *There are many things we do not know.*
>
> *Seekers seek explanation.*
>
> *Four big questions without answer.*
>
> *All to do with creation.*

Wisdom is knowing one does not know everything. Yet, for centuries, atheism has made dogmatic assertions "proving" God is not real that later generations realized were wrong—and this trend has continued to this day.

Modern atheism has at least four empirical (testable) issues it needs to resolve that currently give a much higher probability of having "God" as cause.

Stanza 2

> *How did the cosmos come to be?*
>
> *Fine-tuned for life's emergence!*
>
> *What or who caused the universe?*
>
> *Science and faith's convergence!*

The first empirical question that atheists need to answer is:

"What caused the universe to come into existence?"

Atheism mostly claims "quantum fluctuation" – a characteristic of this universe's spacetime that somehow traversed the infinite singularity to trigger the big bang.

Remarkably, the same people who cannot merge quantum field theory with general relativity, who cannot explain what comprises 95% of the universe's mass and energy by simply calling them "dark matter" and "dark energy," and who have contradictory models for the universe's expansion rate; somehow, confidently claim to know what happened <u>before</u> this universe's time and space existed?

What this means is they are just guessing what caused the universe. They cannot prove anything and have no idea except the belief that God was not involved.

Stanza 3

How did living things come to be?

Living cell's complexity!

How did complex come from simple?

Impossible chemistry!

The second empirical question is:

"What caused life to come into existence?"

Biologists and atheists blithely proclaim life naturally evolved on a prebiotic Earth (*abiogenesis*). Mix some chemicals, throw in some lightning, heat, and ultraviolet rays, and let it simmer for millions of years—and life inevitably emerges.

However, the real experts on developing complex molecules from simpler ones, the synthetic chemists, know this is an impossible process. No known pathways exist to create the components that make up a living cell. They have no idea how carbohydrates, lipids, proteins, and nucleic acids can be formed naturally on a prebiotic Earth, especially before the advent of enzymes to catalyze chemical reactions.

Life arising naturally out of nonliving materials not only cannot be proven, but it also contradicts synthetic chemistry's practices—which comprise of stringent purity and environmental controls as well as experimental and sequential methodology. These are the *opposite* of what happens in nature because contamination, water, sunlight, oxygen, heat, and impurities degrade complex molecules or prevent them from forming.

The artificial creation of the precursors of RNA, amino acids, or lipids is more comparable to the creation of rivets. In contrast, the complexity of a living cell is closer to an airplane. Just because rivets may be used to assemble an airplane does not mean rivets are airplanes.

Anyone who knows how to create life out of nonliving materials will quickly become the richest person who ever lived – because they would have created the foundation for feeding the planet using industrial means, without the need for farming or raising food.

Stanza 4

> *How did modern man come to be?*
>
> *With stunning ability!*
>
> *What's with our superiority?*
>
> *Reason and morality?*

The third empirical question is:

> "What caused anatomically modern humans to come into existence?"

Modern humans (*Homo sapiens sapiens*) are not just incrementally superior to every other hominid or animal, we are qualitatively different. We possess over forty (40) traits and characteristics utterly absent in every other animal and somehow acquired them within just 50,000 to 300,000 years. A "blink of an eye," evolutionarily speaking.

As an example, we are the only species with our posture; who can throw a rock or baseball accurately;

who can create and use fire; speak and use language via different modes; create complex, multi-part and multi-step tools like a spear or bow and arrow; read and write; wear and produce clothing; and dozens of other traits and characteristics.

We have evolutionary evidence going back billions of years with millions of species. Yet, we have never seen just one of these traits and behaviors replicated by an evolutionary change in any other species outside the archaic human Homo sapiens. Not one. And yet, they all appeared in just one genus, within a period too short for these significant evolutionary changes to occur.

It is as if someone or something did some germline genetic modifications to one or more hominids at some point or points in the past hundred thousand years that drastically altered Homo sapiens to create the anatomically modern human *Homo sapiens sapiens*.

One or two genetic mutations are undoubtedly possible, but what kind of mutations explain all of modern human's unique characteristics, especially when there are no precedents in other species despite over 650 million years of animal evolution?

We have no models to show how it can be done. The more we learn about genetics, the harder it is to justify the absence of deliberate design in explaining why we are so different and so superior to every other animal.

If atheists accept the idea that a genetic engineer can intentionally modify specific cells of a species that propagate into the future within a world where random evolution exists, then there is no logical reason God could not do the same to our genetic ancestors.

Although we share the same DNA with every other form of life and are, without a doubt, genetic descendants of hominid ancestors, we are totally and utterly different from everyone else that we might as well be from another planet.

Stanza 5

The New Testament has one voice.

It shouldn't have, but it has!

Many authors, but one message.

Removed by time and distance!

No common editor nor frame.

Correlative components!

Impossible accomplishment.

Great joy to its proponents!

The fourth empirical question is:

"*How did the nine writers of the New Testament's 27 books produce a coherent cosmology comprised of abstract ideas without using a shared frame or harmonizing editor?"*

The New Testament is a frameless, unharmonized, correlative anthology – a testable impossibility. Yet, somehow, at least nine different authors, separated by decades and distance, wrote harmonious and correlative deliverables of abstract ideas that blend into one voice.

That does *not* happen without *external* constraints.

It is human nature for each person to have unique perspectives and views—and these cannot be combined with other understandings without writing within a common frame (style guide, instructions) or employing the help of a harmonizing editor.

And yet, Matthew, Mark, Luke, John, Paul, Peter, the Hebraist, James, and Jude did not have a common frame or set of instructions to follow to ensure their writings were "orthodox." It is as if each writer had unique pieces of a puzzle that, when put together, created a complete picture. Also, the New Testament books were not edited by a joint editor to harmonize their contents.

As an example, if one were to ask nine people to draw <u>parts</u> of a "human-designed structure" on pieces of paper and give them no further details, the pieces would not perfectly fit together to create a seamless whole. Some will draw part of a house, another a car, another an airplane, and so forth.

And yet, the New Testament has a single core cosmology. Somehow, multiple authors produced a correlative anthology without using a common frame or editor.

So unlikely is this accomplishment that I, someone with decades of experience in correlative anthologies like major project execution plans and proposals, estimate the New Testament's single coherent cosmology to be a four-sigma (4σ) event. To say it another way, I believe it is 99.9936% *likely* that something supernatural was associated with its creation. It is not "proof" of God (which I consider a five-sigma event), but it is the next best thing.

Stanza 6

The world owes a great debt to Christ.

Mankind's life is much better!

Tangible benefits to all —

All thanks to his followers!

Foundation of all our science.

Annulment of slavery!

Innate value of all humans.

Real freedom from tyranny!

As mentioned in the Introduction, Christianity was the foundation of the modern countries of Europe and North America. All the world's "civilized" nations share morals and laws that can be traced to Christ's teachings. In fact, Christ's moral teachings created the concept of natural rights and justifies them.

Most inventions and technology that make our lives better owe a debt to the Christians who established modern science hundreds of years ago. Even those who have never been Christian owe so much to Christianity because Christians were the ones who influenced their nations into creating universities and hospitals, educational degrees, libraries, book publishing, sanitation systems, water and wastewater infrastructure, and so forth.

Without Christianity, there would not be any freedom of speech, freedom of and from religion, freedom of travel, freedom of assembly, property rights, and so forth. The world did not get them from Islam, Buddhism, Sikhism, Shintoism, Taoism, the Baha'i, or Hinduism — they came from Christianity and those whose moral compass was guided by it. It is why someone can leave and ridicule the dominant religion without fear in Salt Lake City or Rome – but get killed if done in Mecca.

If Jesus Christ had never existed, there would never have been an England, France, Spain, Germany, or the United States. We would not have the Scientific Method, universal health care, general literacy, social services, or recognition of our natural rights.

The world we know would be a vastly different, uglier, bleaker, and miserable place. Half of our children would still be dying before reaching their fifth year, we would have an average life expectancy of less than 40, and at least a quarter of us will die violent deaths. Most of us would be enslaved farmers ruled by superstition, and only a minority of us will even know how to read.

There is no doubt Jesus has and is continuing to have the most significant positive impact on the world. Everyone has directly benefitted from his influence regardless of country, race, religion, or culture.

Stanza 7

So, come, and meet the real Jesus –

The one who improved your life!

Discover who he truly is.

Why not have eternal life?

God extends an open invitation to all of us: We can have eternal life by following his Son. So why not try it, experience a life of meaning and joy, and the blessings of divine adoption in the next life?

Clarification of the "1. The Pre-Existence of Jesus" Stanzas

1a: Jesus existed before creation

> *In the beginning was the Word.*
>
> *And the Word was with God!*
>
> *He existed before the world.*
>
> *And ere the universe!*

Our cosmology is vastly different than those of the biblical writers. For the first time in history, we can finally understand enigmatic biblical passages that describe Jesus existing before "creation" (i.e., big bang) in a location outside the universe or in another realm.[14]

> "<u>He</u> is the image of the God who has never been seen, and <u>existed before the universe was created</u>. 16 He created the universe. Everything in heaven and earth, everything we see and cannot see, including thrones, powers, rulers, or authorities; he created them all, and

---

[14] The possibility also exists that this reality is a designed world like an advanced video game or simulation while God lives in the "real" world outside it.

they are for him. 17 <u>He existed before the universe</u> and causes it to hold together." **(Holy Bible: Colossians 1:15-17)**

"In the beginning was the Word; the Word existed with God; and the Word was God. 2 <u>He existed with God in the beginning</u>. 3 He created the universe. Nothing exists that he did not create. . . 10 He went and lived on Earth. And even though he created it, the world's inhabitants did not know who he was. . .

14 The Word became flesh and lived among us. We have seen his glory—the glory of the only Son of the Father, full of grace and truth." **(Holy Bible: John 1:1-3,10,14)**

1b: Jesus was "God" by nature

The Son has the Father's nature.

By nature, he is God!

The Son radiates God's glory.

Exact image of God!

Our movement away from deductive inference philosophy to empirical science has allowed us to view "nature" as comparable to science's "species." Jesus is God by nature (belongs to the "God" species), just as he is also a man by nature (belongs to the *Homo sapiens sapiens* species).

So important is the need to understand that the Holy Bible repeatedly describes Jesus to be "God" in addition to being a man that the table below[15] identifies, paraphrases, and provides links to over fifty parallel bibles where the Bible either applies the word "God" to Jesus or describes him to be "God" despite not using the word.

I urge you to compare the paraphrases below to what your personal Bible says in the cited passages. If it is not clear, examine the parallel bibles and biblical commentaries. There is a reason why virtually everyone who understands the Koine Greek language knows that the New Testament teaches Jesus is God.

Table 1: Jesus is God

	JESUS IS GOD	
Passage	Paraphrase Based on Nestle-Aland 28	+50 Parallel Bible Versions
John 1:1	In the beginning was the Word; the Word existed with God; and the Word was God.	https://www.biblegateway.com/verse/en/John%201:1

---

[15] Taken from *Is Jesus "God"?:* Chapter 7.3.

Passage	Paraphrase Based on Nestle-Aland 28	+50 Parallel Bible Versions
	JESUS IS GOD	
John 1:3,10,14	He created the universe—nothing exists that was not created by him … 10 He went and lived on Earth and even though he created it, the Earth's inhabitants did not know who he was … 14 The Word became flesh and lived among us. We have seen his glory—the glory of the only Son of the Father, full of grace and truth.	https://www.biblegateway.com/verse/en/John%201:3
		https://www.biblegateway.com/verse/en/John%201:10
		https://www.biblegateway.com/verse/en/John%201:14
Hebrews 1:8-10	But to the Son he said: "Your throne, O God, will last forever. You rule your kingdom with a scepter of righteousness. 9 You have loved righteousness and	https://www.biblegateway.com/verse/en/hebrews%201:8
		https://www.biblegateway.com/verse/en/hebrews%201:9

	JESUS IS GOD	
Passage	Paraphrase Based on Nestle-Aland 28	+50 Parallel Bible Versions
	hated wickedness. Therefore, O God, your God, has anointed you with the oil of joy above anyone else. . . 10 And in the beginning, you, Lord, laid the foundation of the earth. Your hands created the heavens."	https://www.biblegateway.com/verse/en/hebrews%201:10
Philippians 2:5-11	Have the same attitude Jesus Christ had: 6 Although having the same nature as God, he did not think to forcefully cling to his equality with God, 7 but emptied himself of it and took upon him the nature of a slave and became human. 8 As a mortal man, he humbled himself and	https://www.biblegateway.com/verse/en/Philippians%202:5
		https://www.biblegateway.com/verse/en/Philippians%202:6
		https://www.biblegateway.com/verse/en/Philippians%202:7

HYMN STANZA CLARIFICATIONS | 111

	JESUS IS GOD	
Passage	Paraphrase Based on Nestle-Aland 28	+50 Parallel Bible Versions
	was so obedient to the Father's will that he stooped to die the utterly degrading death on the cross.	https://www.biblegateway.com/verse/en/Philippians%202:8
	9 This is why God elevated him higher than anything possible and made his name more exalted than any other name.	https://www.biblegateway.com/verse/en/Philippians%202:9
	10 And at the mention of Jesus's name, every knee in heaven, on earth, and in the underworld shall bend,	https://www.biblegateway.com/verse/en/Philippians%202:10
	11 and everyone will concede that Jesus Christ is Lord, to the glory of God the Father.	https://www.biblegateway.com/verse/en/Philippians%202:11
Colossians 1:12-22	Giving thanks to the Father, the one who certified us to share the inheritance of Christ's	https://www.biblegateway.com/verse/en/Colossians%201:12

JESUS IS GOD			
Passage	Paraphrase Based on Nestle-Aland 28	+50 Parallel Bible Versions
	true followers in the light. 13 He has rescued us from the subjugation of darkness and resettled us to the kingdom of his beloved Son, 14 in whom we have been redeemed and had our sins forgiven.	https://www.biblegateway.com/verse/en/Colossians%201:13
		https://www.biblegateway.com/verse/en/Colossians%201:14
	15 He is the image of the God who has never been seen, and existed before the universe was created. 16 He created the universe. Everything in heaven and earth, everything we see and cannot see, including thrones, powers, rulers, or authorities; he created them all, and they are for him. 17 He existed before the universe and	https://www.biblegateway.com/verse/en/Colossians%201:15
		https://www.biblegateway.com/verse/en/Colossians%201:16
		https://www.biblegateway.com/verse/en/Colossians%201:17
		https://www.biblegateway.com/

JESUS IS GOD

Passage	Paraphrase Based on Nestle-Aland 28	+50 Parallel Bible Versions
	causes it to hold together.	verse/en/Colossians%201:18
	18 And he is the head of the body, which is the church. He is the beginning and the firstborn from the dead so that he might have supremacy over the universe. 19 God was pleased that all his fulness dwelt in Jesus.	https://www.biblegateway.com/verse/en/Colossians%201:19
		https://www.biblegateway.com/verse/en/Colossians%201:20
	20 And through Jesus, God reconciled the universe to himself, whether things on earth or in the heavens—by making peace through Jesus's blood on the cross.	https://www.biblegateway.com/verse/en/Colossians%201:21
	21 You were once alienated from God, with a hostile mind because of your evil actions. 22 But now, Jesus has reconciled	https://www.biblegateway.com/verse/en/Colossians%201:22

JESUS IS GOD		
Passage	Paraphrase Based on Nestle-Aland 28	+50 Parallel Bible Versions
	you in his flesh through his death, to present you to God, holy, unblemished, and beyond reproach.	
Hebrews 1:2-3	And now, God has spoken to us through his Son in these last days. God has given the universe to him as an inheritance, and created it through him. 3 The Son radiates God's glory and is the exact copy of the very essence of God. He sustains the universe by the power of his word. After he made the purification for sins, he sat down on the right-hand side of the majestic God in heaven!	https://www.biblegateway.com/verse/en/Hebrews%201:2 https://www.biblegateway.com/verse/en/Hebrews%201:3
2 Corinthians 8:9	You know the grace of our Lord Jesus Christ:	https://www.biblegateway.com/

HYMN STANZA CLARIFICATIONS | 115

	JESUS IS GOD	
Passage	Paraphrase Based on Nestle-Aland 28	+50 Parallel Bible Versions
	Although he was rich, he became poor for your sakes, so that you may become rich through his poverty.	verse/en/2Corinthians%208:9
1 Corinthians 8:6	To us, there is only one God, the Father, the originator of the universe and for whom we live; and there is one Lord Jesus Christ, the creator of the universe and creator of humankind.	https://www.biblegateway.com/verse/en/1corinthians%208:6
John 1:18	No one has ever seen God; he has been revealed by the only God who is at the Father's side.	https://www.biblegateway.com/verse/en/john%201:18
John 5:26	Just as the Father has life within himself, so has he also given the Son to have life within himself.	https://www.biblegateway.com/verse/en/john%205:26

\multicolumn{3}{c}{**JESUS IS GOD**}
Passage	Paraphrase Based on Nestle-Aland 28	+50 Parallel Bible Versions
John 20:28	Thomas exclaimed to him, "My Lord and my God!"	https://www.biblegateway.com/verse/en/john%2020:28
Acts 20:28	Guard yourselves and the flock that the Holy Spirit entrusted to you. Feed the church of God, which he paid for with his own blood.	https://www.biblegateway.com/verse/en/acts%2020:28
Romans 9:5	Theirs are the patriarchs (Abraham, Isaac, and Jacob) and of whose lineage Christ became flesh. Christ, who is God and rules over the universe, is blessed forever. Amen.	https://www.biblegateway.com/verse/en/romans%209:5
2 Thessalonians 1:12	So that the name of our Lord Jesus may be glorified in you and you in him, according	https://www.biblegateway.com/verse/en/2thessalonians%201:12

HYMN STANZA CLARIFICATIONS | 117

Passage	Paraphrase Based on Nestle-Aland 28	+50 Parallel Bible Versions
	JESUS IS GOD	
	to the grace of our God and Lord Jesus Christ.	
Titus 2:13	Looking for the blessed hope and manifestation of the glory of the great God and Savior Jesus Christ.	https://www.biblegateway.com/verse/en/titus%202:13
2 Peter 1:1	Simon Peter, a servant and apostle of Jesus Christ, writing to those who share the same precious faith through the righteousness of Jesus Christ, our God and Savior.	https://www.biblegateway.com/verse/en/2peter%201:1
1 John 5:20	We know the Son of God came and gave us understanding so that we may know him who is true. We are in him who is true—in his Son, Jesus Christ. He is the true God and is life eternal.	https://www.biblegateway.com/verse/en/1john%205:20

JESUS IS GOD		
Passage	Paraphrase Based on Nestle-Aland 28	+50 Parallel Bible Versions
2 Corinthians 4:4	The god of this world has blinded the minds of unbelievers so that they cannot see the light of the gospel of the glorious Christ, who is in the image of God.	https://www.biblegateway.com/verse/en/2cor%204:4
Revelation 22:6,16	And he said unto me, "Everything you have heard is reliable and true. The Lord God of the prophets sent his angel to show his servants the things that are about to occur." . . . 16 I, Jesus, have sent my angel to witness to you of these things for the churches. I am the root and descendant of David, the bright morning star.	https://www.biblegateway.com/verse/en/revelation%2022:6
		https://www.biblegateway.com/verse/en/revelation%2022:16

	JESUS IS GOD	
Passage	Paraphrase Based on Nestle-Aland 28	+50 Parallel Bible Versions
Isaiah 9:6	For a child will be born to us—a son will be given. He will rule the government and will be called the Wonderful Counselor, the Mighty God, the Father of Eternity, and the Prince of Peace!	https://www.biblegateway.com/verse/en/isaiah%209:6
Micah 5:2	But you, Bethlehem Ephratah, even though you are tiny among the people of Judah, out of you shall come the one who is destined to rule over Israel – and whose origins are from the beginning, from the days of eternity.	https://www.biblegateway.com/verse/en/micah%205:2

1c: Jesus possessed glory before his birth

> *He had glory ere creation.*
>
> *He shared God's glory!*
>
> *He gave up his equality.*
>
> *He emptied his glory!*

Jesus was honored as the Son of God and as one who is "God" by nature before this universe came into existence. He gave up that glory and honor when he decided to become a lowly human.

> *"Now, Father, glorify me with yourself and <u>restore the glory I shared with you before the world's creation</u>. . . 22 I gave them the glory you gave me so that they may be one just as we are one. . . 24 Father, I want those you gave me to be with me where I am. I want them to see <u>the glory you gave me because you already loved me before the world's creation</u>."* **(Holy Bible: John 17:5,22,24)**

1d: Jesus was foreordained to be the Savior before the Earth was created

> *He was foreordained to atone –*
>
> *Before the world was made!*
>
> *He was ordained to save mankind,*
>
> *Before the earth was laid!*

HYMN STANZA CLARIFICATIONS | 121

Jesus was foreordained to perform the Atonement (the Fall's annulment) before this Earth was even made. This means if he was foreordained to atone, then Adam had to be foreordained to Fall for the Atonement to make sense. Thus, Adam's Fall (the introduction of death, sin, moral weakness, and experience of trials) was not a cosmic accident that an all-knowing God did not anticipate. The Fall, although planned, had to be <u>freely</u> done by man for the Atonement to be valid.

> *"So that the times of refreshment will come from the presence of the Lord, and <u>he shall send Jesus Christ, who was foreordained for you</u>."* (**Holy Bible: Acts 3:20**)

> *"As you know, gold and silver were not used to pay your ransom from the futile life you received from your ancestors, 19 but with the incalculably valuable blood of <u>Christ, the</u> unblemished and spotless <u>Lamb of God</u>, 20 <u>who was chosen before the world was created</u>, and was revealed in these last days for your sake."* (**Holy Bible: 1 Peter 1:18-20**)

1e: Jesus came from heaven before birth

> *He came from heaven before birth.*
>
> *The Son came from heaven!*
>
> *He gave up heaven to come here.*
>
> *God's only Son left heaven!*

The pre-mortal Jesus lived in heaven before he was born on this world and returned to heaven after his resurrection. This "heaven" already existed before this universe was made, which means it is a realm that exists external to this universe (either another universe or something else we cannot even conceive).

> *"For <u>the bread of God is the bread who comes down from heaven</u> and gives life to the world. . . 38 <u>God sent me down from heaven</u> to do what he wants, not what I want.*
>
> *50 All who eat this bread from heaven will never die. 51 <u>I am the living bread that came down from heaven</u>. Whoever eats this bread will live forever. The bread that I give for the life of humanity is my flesh. . . 58 <u>This is the bread from heaven</u>. Unlike your ancestors who ate manna and died, whoever eats this bread will live forever. . .*
>
> *62 <u>What if you were to see the Son of Man ascend to where he was before?</u>"* **(Holy Bible: John 6:33,38, 50-51, 58, 62)**
>
> *"<u>He who comes from above is greater than all others</u>. Those who come from the earth belong to the earth and can only speak of earthly things. <u>He who comes from heaven is greater than everyone else</u>. 32 He tells them of what he saw and heard, yet no one believes his testimony!"* **(Holy Bible: John 3:31-32)**

1f: Jesus came from the Father before birth

Jesus came from God the Father.

Thank you, God, for your Son!

Jesus was sent by his Father.

Thank you, O Holy One!

The pre-mortal Jesus came from the Father (who dwells in "heaven") when he became human. Jesus was not a thought but had an actual existence as the only "Son of God" who was also "God" by nature before becoming human.

> *"Jesus then told them, 'I am only going to be with you for a bit longer, and <u>then I am going to the one who sent me to earth</u>. 34 You will look for me but will not find me. You cannot go to where I am going.'"* (**Holy Bible: John 7:33-34**)

> *"Jesus said to them, 'If God were your Father, you would love me because <u>I came from God. I am not here on my own accord—he sent me.</u>'"* (**Holy Bible: John 8:42**)

1g: Jesus was the Old Testament God[16]

> *Jesus is the Lord of Israel.*
>
> *He is the Great I AM!*
>
> *God's only Son is the Lord of lords.*
>
> *He is the King of kings!*

The dominant figure of the Old Testament was the Hebrew God, YHWH (pronounced "Jehovah" or "Yahweh"). The dominant figure of the New Testament was Jesus Christ.

Jesus was frequently identified as the "Son of God," which was understood by his contemporary Jews to mean he was the "Son of Jehovah" since they viewed "God" to be "Jehovah." To this day, many think the Bible describes Jesus as the Son of the Old Testament God, Jehovah.

But there is a problem with this understanding because the New Testament writers repeatedly and consistently referred to Jesus using words and descriptions that were solely used to refer to Jehovah in the Hebrew Scriptures instead of using language that treated him as the Son of Jehovah.

---

[16] This subsection is copied from *Is Jesus "God"?*: Chapter 7.2.

HYMN STANZA CLARIFICATIONS | 125

These are not just a few instances where one can dismiss them as coincidences. Eight of the nine New Testament writers (James excepted) did this around 90 times, paralleling 80 Old Testament locations.

The word selection was intentional – they alluded to Jesus being Jehovah without explicitly saying "Jesus is Jehovah" explicitly.

Why did they not just say it out loud? Because if they had done so, Christianity could have never been established due to the cultural practice of the Jews of that era. They violently reacted to anything they perceived demeaned Jehovah, such as the utterance of his name or bringing down his glory to the human level. It would have been impossible for Jesus to get any followers (who were all Jews), and he would have been killed a lot sooner. His self-reference as the "I AM" (John 8:58-59) was sufficient for the Jews to try to kill him; how much more if he blatantly went around saying he was Jehovah made flesh?

Given the first-century milieu, it is a miracle that the New Testament contains the passages it does concerning the deity of Jesus Christ.

Although certain Christian denominations reject Jesus as Jehovah, the parallels are clear and indisputable:

Table 2: Jesus is Jehovah

JESUS IS JEHOVAH (YHWH)		
Description	**Old Testament (Jehovah)**	**New Testament (Jesus Christ)**
1. I AM	Ex 3:14; Deut 32:39; Isa 41:4; Isa 43:10; Isa 46:4	John 8:58; John 8:24,28; John 13:19; John 18:5-8
2. SAVIOR	Hos 13:4; Isa 43:11	Luke 2:11; Acts 4:10-12; 1 Jn 4:14-15
3. REDEEMER	Isa 43:14; Isa 44:24; Isa 49:26; Isa 54:5	Gal 3:13; Eph 1:7; Col 1:13-14; Tit 2:13-14
4. PIERCED	Zech 12:10	John 19:34-37; Rev 1:7
5. FIRST/LAST	Isa 44:6; Isa 48:12	Rev 1:8,17-18; Rev 22:12-16
6. CREATOR	Gen 2:4; Job 38:1-4; Ps 8:1-3; Ps 102:25; Isa 44:24; Isa 45:11-12; Isa 66:2	John 1:1,3,10,14; Col 1:13-17; Heb 1:10
7. HUSBAND / GROOM	Isa 54:5; Isa 62:5; Jer 3:1-2; Hos 2:16	Luke 5:34-35; Rev 19:7-8; Rev 21:9

HYMN STANZA CLARIFICATIONS | 127

JESUS IS JEHOVAH (YHWH)		
Description	Old Testament (Jehovah)	New Testament (Jesus Christ)
8. SENDS PROPHETS	2 Kg 17:13; 2 Chr 36:15-16	Matt 23:34
9. SAVES FROM DEATH	Hos 13:14	1 Cor 15:20-22
10. JUDGE	1 Chr 16:33; Ps 9:7; Ps 50:6; Ps 96:13	Matt 16:27; John 5:22; 2 Cor 5:10
11. SHEPHERD	Ps 23:1; Ezek 34:11-16	John 10:14-16; 1 Pet 2:25; 1 Pet 5:4
12. LORD OF LORDS	Deut 10:17; Ps 136:3	1 Tim 6:14-15; Rev 17:14; Rev 19:13-16
13. EVERY KNEE SHALL BOW UNTO HIM	Isa 45:23	Phil 2:10-11
14. SEEN BY ISAIAH	Isa 6:1-10	John 12:39-41; John 1:18
15. PRECEDED BY VOICE IN THE DESERT	Isa 40:3-9; Mal 3:1	Matt 3:3,11-12; Matt 11:10; Luke 1:76; Luke 3:4-6; Luke 7:27; John 1:6-8,15-36

JESUS IS JEHOVAH (YHWH)		
Description	Old Testament (Jehovah)	New Testament (Jesus Christ)
16. CALL UPON HIS NAME	Ps 99:6; Ps 116:13,17; Isa 12:4; Joel 2:32; Zeph 3:9; Zech 13:8-9	Acts 7:59; Acts 9:5,13-14,17,21; Rom 10:9,13; 1 Cor 1:2; Rev 22:20
17. ROCK	Ex 13:21-22; Deut 32:3-4; Ps 62:6-7; Ps 118:22; Isa 8:13-14	Acts 4:10-12; Rom 9:33; 1 Cor 10:1-4; 1 Pet 2:4-8
18. HOLY ONE	Isa 43:14-15; Hos 11:9; Hab 1:12	Mark 1:24; Acts 3:14; 1 Jn 2:20
19. OUR RIGHTEOUSNESS	Jer 23:5-6	1 Cor 1:30
20. GATHERS LIKE A HEN GATHERS HER CHICKS	Ps 31:20; Ps 32:7; Ps 57:1; Ps 91:1-10; Isa 31:5	Matt 23:37-38; Luke 13:34-35
21. HIS BREATH SLAYS THE WICKED	Job 4:9; Isa 11:4	2 Thes 2:8

JESUS IS JEHOVAH (YHWH)		
Description	Old Testament (Jehovah)	New Testament (Jesus Christ)
22. WILL RETURN WITH HIS HOLY ONES	Zech 14:5; Deut 33:2	Jude 1:14; 1 Tim 6:14; 2 Tim 4:1; Tit 2:13; 1 Thes 3:13
23. PRESERVES ALL THINGS	Neh 9:6; Ps 148:5-6	Col 1:17; Heb 1:3
24. GONE UP/COME DOWN WITH A SHOUT, WITH TRUMPETS BLARING	Ps 47:5	1 Thes 4:16
25. THOU SHALT NOT TEMPT THE LORD THY GOD	Deut 6:16	Matt 4:7; 1 Cor 10:9
26. WALKS ON THE SEA	Job 9:8	Matt 14:25-33; Mark 6:48-51; John 6:19-21
27. CALMS WIND AND WAVES	Ps 65:5-8	Matt 8:23-27
28. DAY OF THE LORD	Isa 2:12; Jer 46:10; Ezek 30:3; Joel 1:15; Obad 1:15;	Acts 2:20; 1 Cor 1:7-8; 1 Cor 5:5; 2 Cor 1:14; 1 Thes 5:2; 2 Pet 3:10

JESUS IS JEHOVAH (YHWH)		
Description	Old Testament (Jehovah)	New Testament (Jesus Christ)
	Zeph 1:7,14; Mal 4:5	
29. HIS THRONE IS FOREVER	Ps 45:6-7	Heb 1:8-9
30. LAID EARTH'S FOUNDATION	Ps 102:24-27	Heb 1:10-12
31. RECEIVES OUR SPIRITS	Ps 31:5	Acts 7:59
32. ANGELS WORSHIP HIM	Deut 32:43 LXX; Ps 97:7 LXX	Heb 1:6

To give just one of over 30 parallel descriptions, the Old Testament said the entity who created our reality was Jehovah. He was the one who laid the Earth's foundation, and it was his hands that did the work (Gen 2:4; Job 38:1-4; Ps 8:1-3; Ps 102:25; Isa 44:24; Isa 45:11-12; Isa 66:2). The New Testament parallels this by stating, repeatedly, that the pre-mortal Jesus was the being who created our reality (John 1:3,10,14; Col 1:13-17; Heb 1:8-10; Heb 2:10) under his Father's instructions (1 Cor 8:6; Heb 1:2-3; Rev 3:14). His hands did the work (Heb 1:8-10).

There is no doubt that both actors are credited with both creations, which means they are the same entity if the Old Testament and New Testament are equally Scripture. Consequently, Jesus is the pre-mortal Jehovah.

The "Big Picture"

As shown above, the Holy Bible clearly describes Jesus Christ as God by nature while separate from the entity known as "God" or his Father. After Jesus performed his infinite substitutionary sacrifice, the Atonement, the Father rewarded him with this entire universe as his eternal inheritance (Matt 11:27; John 3:35; Heb 1:2; Heb 2:10; Matt 28:18; John 13:3; Rom 9:5; Col 1:16-20; John 16:15; John 17:10; Matt 19:28; Acts 10:36; 1 Cor 15:25-28; Eph 1:10,20-23).

The Holy Bible describes Jesus as the most important figure in our past, present, and future. He was the Creator of the universe and Earth. He is our Savior and Judge. He is our Redeemer who will turn his true disciples over to the Father to share in God's very nature, oneness, and mutual indwelling by divine adoption. He causes us to become the heirs of God and his fellow-heirs who will rule over the universe forever.

If Jesus were the Creator of the universe and the Earth and is the central figure in every aspect of our reality, then why would the Father be the Hebrew God (YHWH) during the Old Testament era and restrict his direct involvement with humans to only that era and *nowhere else?*

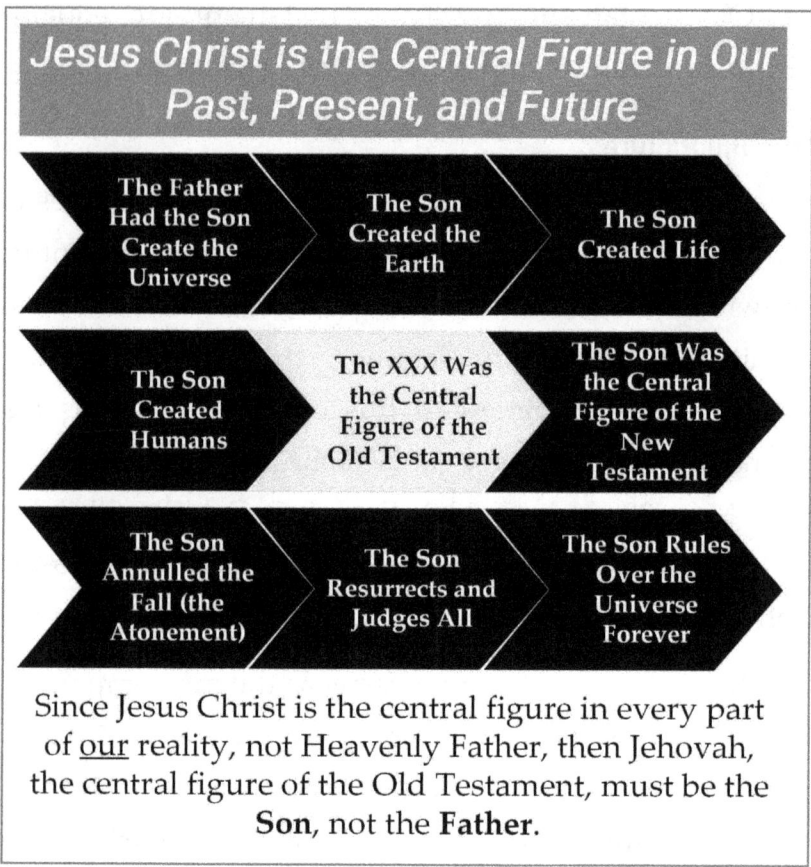

Since Jesus Christ is the central figure in every part of <u>our</u> reality, not Heavenly Father, then Jehovah, the central figure of the Old Testament, must be the **Son**, not the **Father**.

The Son is our primary interface with the Father for all things relative to *this* universe. Everything that occurs within this universe is within the Son's dominion. He is the gatekeeper between his Father and all humans (Rev 7:17; John 14:6; 1 Tim 2:5; Acts 4:10-12).

This means that the revelation of the Father is <u>*new,*</u> and the Bible only knew about him because Jehovah told us about him after he became a mortal human two thousand years ago.

The Son always talked about his Father, which most Jews assumed, incorrectly, was the Israelite God, Jehovah. They did not realize that their God, Jehovah, became human flesh and walked amongst them as Jesus Christ.

The New Testament gave us something new: The ability to communicate with the Father through his Son in prayer (John 14:13-14; John 16:23-24; Eph 5:20; Col 3:17 cf. Matt 6:6-13) and the insight that Jehovah (that is, Jesus) has a Father. Of course, Jesus told us that the Father is his God and our God, but these statements do not deny his nature as "God," any more than one can deny their nature to be "man" just because someone else is named "Man."

While fully human, the Son also is fully "God" and shares oneness and mutual indwelling with the Father. The Father gave the Son all authority to act in his name. Any honor given to one is given to the other due to the Son representing the Father (John 5:23; Luke 10:16; John 15:23-24; 1 John 2:23) and innate equality (Hebrews 1:3; John 5:17-18).

It then is perfectly acceptable to describe Jesus as the "Son of God" in one sense and as "God" in another sense, and even as "our God" in a third sense. In like manner, he can be considered "Jehovah" in one sense and the "Son of Jehovah" in another.

Unfortunately, some pick and choose biblical passages to justify a belief while ignoring those that conflict with the doctrine. This practice puts their ideology above the Holy Bible – a dangerous thing.

The correct action is to take the biblical passages as a whole and harmonize the different passages to get the "big picture" message. After all, around 90 New Testament "Jesus" passages are deliberately paralleled with Old Testament "Jehovah" passages. One cannot sweep them under the rug and pretend they do not exist.

Using this comprehensive approach allows us to conclude that according to the Holy Bible:

- Jesus is God by nature (he is "God" by nature just as we are "human" by nature) and by title (we can refer to him as our God just as we can consider the Father to be our God as well due to their oneness and mutual indwelling)

- Jesus is the Son of God by title (he is recognized as the "Son" of the entity known as "God")

- Jesus is Jehovah by title (he is the entity in the Old Testament known as "Jehovah")

- Jesus is the Son of Jehovah by title (he is recognized as the "Son" of the entity known as "Jehovah" when used as a synonym for "God")

As a result, either the Father or the Son can be called "Jehovah Elohim" or "LORD God."

If Jesus can be called "God" and the "Son of God" without contradiction, then he can also be called "Jehovah" and the "Son of Jehovah" as well.

If Jesus had never told us about the Father, then the New Testament would have described Jesus as Jehovah becoming human flesh instead of God becoming flesh.

There is no doubt that the Old Testament Jehovah and the New Testament Jesus are the same person.

1h: Jesus is God's Only Begotten Son

God gave his only Son for us.

His great work had begun!

God's Son obeyed his Father's will.

Thank you, Lord, for your Son!

The Bible frequently describes Jesus as God's "Only Begotten Son," indicating a special relationship between Father and Son that does not exist between the Father and any other entity.

"God loved humankind so much that <u>he gave up his only Son</u>. Whoever believes in him shall not perish but have eternal life." (**Holy Bible: John 3:16**)

"God showed his love toward us by sending <u>his only Son into the world</u> so that we might live through him. 10 This is real love: Not that we loved God, but because he loved us—and <u>sent his Son to be the appeasing sacrifice for our sins!</u>" (**Holy Bible: 1 John 4:9-10**)

"God did what the Law of Moses was incapable of doing due to the weakness of flesh: <u>God condemned sin in the flesh by sending his own Son to become flesh</u>. . . 32 Since <u>God did not spare his own Son but gave him up for our sakes</u>, there is then nothing that he would not also give us." (**Holy Bible: Romans 8:3,32**)

Clarification of the "2. Jesus Mutually Indwells With the Father" Stanzas

2a: The Father, Son, and Holy Spirit share a common space

Father, Son, and Holy Spirit–

They dwell in each other!

Whether by will or innately,

Within one another!

Jesus repeatedly claimed he dwelt in the Father, and his Father dwelt in him. Yet, simultaneously, his words and actions showed they were not the same entity but were distinct from one another and had their own personalities.

> "But if I do the work, even though you do not believe me, at least believe the works, so that you will know that <u>the Father is in me, and I am in him</u>." **(Holy Bible: John 10:38)**

> "Do you not believe that <u>I am in the Father, and the Father is in me</u>? The words I say are not from me but <u>from the Father who dwells in me</u>. 11 <u>Believe me when I say I am in the Father and the Father is in me</u> or at least believe because of my work. . . 20 <u>On that day, you will understand that I am in my Father</u>, and you are in me, and I am in you." **(Holy Bible: John 14:10-11,20)**

> "That they may be one <u>just as you are in me and I in you</u>. May they be in us so that the world may believe that you sent me. . . 23 I in them and <u>you in me</u>, so that they may become perfectly united. The world will then know that you sent me and loved them just as you loved me." **(Holy Bible: John 17:21,23)**

The Son is not the Father, nor is the Father the Son. Stephen saw two distinct forms while he was being killed (Acts 7:55-56), and Jesus repeatedly described his Father "in heaven" while he was spatially separated from him while on Earth.

But somehow, through a process we do not understand, these beings who simultaneously straddle this universe and an external realm are literally within each other's three-dimensional[17] space from our perspective. This explains Jesus Christ's anguish when the Father withdrew from him when he was hanging on the cross (*"My God, my God, why have you forsaken me?"* [Mark 15:34]). The Father withdrew from that indwelling so that Jesus could complete the sacrifice by himself.[18]

Furthermore, the Holy Bible only describes the mutual indwelling—it does *not* say that this state is the default natural condition of God or done by will or mutual consent.

The fourth-century developers of the Trinity[19] believed the mutual indwelling was ontologically dimensionally innate and used specific Greek

---

[17] For lack of a better description.

[18] While the parallel with Psalms 22 is undeniable, it is critical that Jesus Christ complete the Atonement by himself, without any help from his Father. Since the Father's presence within the Son gave comfort and strength, it would not have been a legitimate substitution if the Father stayed within his Son.

[19] Athanasius of Alexandria and the Three Cappadocians (Basil the Great, Gregory of Nyssa, and Gregory of Nazianzus) are primarily responsible for the dominant Trinity formula used today.

philosophical ideas (most notably, Neoplatonism) to frame the biblical concepts to arrive at a deductive theory that became dogma despite being untestable.

But modern science's inductive process triumphed over the earlier deductive model centuries ago as the latter failed to make empirical sense of the world. This now allows for a reexamination of the biblical mutual indwelling without employing the now-obsolete theoretical frame.

Thus, from the modern scientific perspective using inductive reasoning onto the biblical text, the divine mutual indwelling is more likely to be a function of divine will (i.e., "The Father and Son can literally occupy the same three-dimensional space *if they want*, just as the glorified Jesus can be in multiple places at the same time *if he wants*").

This latter position assumes ontological separation is the natural state of the Father and Son to preserve the individuality of each person, and to stay true to the face value reading of numerous biblical passages denoting spatial separation, most notably when Jesus felt the Father *leave* him while he was on the cross (Matthew 27:46; Mark 15:34). This would have been impossible if the mutual indwelling is ontologically innate. It also explains how the *same* oneness and mutual indwelling are shared with us (John 15:1-11; John 17:11,21-23), creatures of obvious ontological separation from each other, since we have our own personal space.

2b: Jesus is in the image of God

> *Christ is in the image of God.*
>
> *God's glory on his face!*
>
> *He is an exact duplicate –*
>
> *Of God's very essence!*

Whatever the Father is, the Son is the exact duplicate. Whatever makes God "God" makes the Son "God" as well.

> *"In the beginning was the Word; the Word existed with God; and <u>the Word was God</u>."* **(Holy Bible: John 1:1)**

> *"<u>He is the image of the God who has never been seen</u>, and existed before the universe was created."* **(Holy Bible: Colossians 1:15)**

> *"And now, God has spoken to us through his Son in these last days. God has given the universe to him as an inheritance, and created it through him. 3 <u>The Son radiates God's glory and is the exact copy of the very essence of God</u>. He sustains the universe by the power of his word. After he made the purification for sins, he sat down on the right-hand side of the majestic God in heaven!"* **(Holy Bible: Hebrews 1:2-3)**

HYMN STANZA CLARIFICATIONS | 141

2c: Jesus is in the Father; the Father is in him

The Son is in God the Father.

The Father's in the Son!

They indwell in one another.

Always within each one!

Jesus said:

> "Do you not believe that <u>I am in the Father, and the Father is in me</u>? The words I say are not from me but from <u>the Father who dwells in me</u>. 11 Believe me when I say <u>I am in the Father and the Father is in me</u> or at least believe because my work. . . 20 On that day, you will understand that <u>I am in my Father</u>, and you are in me, and I am in you." **(Holy Bible: John 14:10-11,20)**

Interestingly, Jesus described this mutual indwelling as being extended to those who are his genuine followers.

2d: Jesus is one with the Father

The Son is one with the Father.

Father and Son are one!

Jesus said God was one with him.

A oneness with the Son!

Jesus said:

> "<u>The Father and I are one</u>." **(Holy Bible: John 10:30)**

> "Holy Father, I am about to leave this world and go to you, but they are staying in this world. Protect them by the power of your name so that <u>they may be one as we are one</u>. . . 21 That <u>they may be one just as you are in me and I in you</u>. May they be in us so that the world may believe that you sent me. 22 I gave them the glory you gave me so that <u>they may be one just as we are one</u>. 23 I in them and you in me, so that they may become perfectly united. The world will then know that you sent me and loved them just as you loved me." (**Holy Bible: John 17:11,21-23**)

Just as with mutual indwelling, the Son's oneness with the Father is extended to his true followers.

2e: The Father is glorified in Jesus

> *The Father glorifies the Son.*
>
> *Christ gives glory to God!*
>
> *God honors Christ within himself.*
>
> *Son's glorified by God!*

Jesus said:

> "The time has come for the Son of Man's glorification, and <u>God is glorified in him</u>. 32 If God is glorified in him, <u>God will glorify the Son of Man within himself</u>, and shall immediately glorify him." (**Holy Bible: John 13:31-32**)

2f: Jesus is equal to the Father

> *The Son's equal to the Father.*
>
> *Eternal equality!*
>
> *Equal praise to Father and Son.*
>
> *Equal eternally!*

Jesus is equal to the Father in several ways:

(i) By nature

> *"But Jesus answered, 'My Father is constantly working, and so am I.' 18 When they heard this, the Jews sought all the more to have him killed because not only did he break the Sabbath by working, but he also called God his Father, making himself equal to God."* **(Holy Bible: John 5:17-18)**

> *"The Son radiates God's glory and is the exact copy of the very essence of God. He sustains the universe by the power of his word. After he made the purification for sins, he sat down on the right-hand side of the majestic God in heaven!"* **(Holy Bible: Hebrews 1:3)**

(ii) By Honor

> *"So that everyone may honor the Son just as they honor the Father. Whoever does not honor the Son is not honoring the one who sent him, the Father."* **(Holy Bible: John 5:23)**

(iii) Self-recognition (using *"erotao"* instead of *"aiteo"*)[20]

> *"And I will <u>ask</u> the Father to give you another Agent like myself, to be with you forever."* (**Holy Bible: John 14:16**)

> *"On that day, you will ask in my name. I do not speak of <u>asking</u> the Father for you."* (**Holy Bible: John 16:26**)

Heavenly Father is greater than his Son (John 14:28) by position and rank; not by nature – just as a general is greater than a captain despite being equally human.

2g: The fulness of God was in Jesus's body

> *God's fulness dwelt in Christ's body.*
>
> *God's fulness in his flesh!*
>
> *God's fulness was in his body.*
>
> *God's fulness in Christ's flesh!*

All of God's "fulness" dwelt within Christ. This can be understood in several ways. Most notably, all that makes

---

[20] This example is absent in English but present in the Koine Greek of the New Testament. Suffice to say when Jesus described himself asking the Father, he uses "erotao" – a word where the petitioner is on an equal footing to the one being asked, never "aiteo" where the petitioner is in an inferior position. (W.E. Vine. *Expository Dictionary of New Testament Words:* "Ask")

God "God" was in the physical body of Jesus, or the Father literally dwelt within the physical body of Jesus.

"God was pleased that <u>all his fulness dwelt in Jesus</u>." **(Holy Bible: Colossians 1:19)**

"<u>All of God's fulness dwells in the body of Jesus</u>." **(Holy Bible: Colossians 2:9)**

2h: One sees the Father when looking at Jesus

To see one, one sees the other.

Jesus, show me your face!

To see him, one sees the Father.

Father, give us your grace!

Jesus said:

"Philip, after all this time we have been together, do you not know me by now? <u>Anyone who has seen me has seen the Father.</u> How then can you ask me to show him to you? 10 Do you not believe that I am in the Father, and the Father is in me? The words I say are not from me but from the Father who dwells in me. 11 Believe me when I say I am in the Father and the Father is in me or at least believe because of my work." **(Holy Bible: John 14:9-11)**

The Father and Son dwelt within each other. We cannot conceive of what this looks like, but whatever it is, we can enjoy the same oneness and mutual indwelling with them by divine adoption (John 17:11,21-23).

Clarification of the "3. Jesus is the Almighty Creator" Stanzas

3a: The Father created the universe through Jesus

> *God made the universe through Christ.*
>
> *Sire ordered; Son obeyed!*
>
> *This reality came to be –*
>
> *Father designed; Son made!*

Heavenly Father ordered his Only Begotten Son, Jesus, to create this vast, inconceivably huge universe:

> "To us, there is only one God, <u>the Father, the originator of the universe</u> and for whom we live; and <u>there is one Lord Jesus Christ, the creator of the universe and creator of humankind.</u>" **(Holy Bible: 1 Corinthians 8:6)**

3b: Jesus created the universe

> *God's only Son made the cosmos.*
>
> *Every planet and star!*
>
> *He made the big bang's time and space.*
>
> *And all things near and far!*

Modern cosmology has allowed us to conceptualize just what the Bible means when it describes all reality as being created by Jesus Christ:

> *"He is the image of the God who has never been seen, and existed before the universe was created. 16 <u>He created the universe. Everything in heaven and earth, everything we see and cannot see</u>, including thrones, powers, rulers, or authorities; <u>he created them all</u>, and they are for him."* **(Holy Bible: Colossians 1:15-16)**

3c: Nothing exists that was not created by Jesus

Nothing exists without Christ's word.

There's naught he didn't make!

Everything in heaven and earth —

All things he did create!

Jesus is described as follows:

> *"<u>He created the universe. Nothing exists that he did not create</u>. . . 10 He went and lived on Earth. And even though he created it, the world's inhabitants did not know who he was. . . 14 The Word became flesh and lived among us. We have seen his glory—the glory of the only Son of the Father, full of grace and truth."* **(Holy Bible: John 1:3,10,14)**

3d: Jesus sustains the universe

> *Jesus sustains the universe.*
>
> *He keeps it together!*
>
> *By the power of our Lord's word –*
>
> *He holds it together!*

The Bible describes Jesus to be the active source of the universe's fundamental integrity:

> "<u>He existed before the universe and causes it to hold together</u>." **(Holy Bible: Colossians 1:17)**
>
> "<u>He sustains the universe by the power of his word</u>." **(Holy Bible: Hebrews 1:3)**

Jesus is the reason the universe appears "fine-tuned" for the emergence of the complex molecules called "life." This support is a <u>continuous</u> process, which implies his will or effort is the only thing keeping the universe's integrity together.

Pondering the implications of actively sustaining the universe's integrity means Christ has absolute control over every portion of the universe and can modify any part of it at any time to his whim. He can form worlds and stars by merely commanding matter to coalesce or even order them to disappear. He can change elements from one to another by simply telling atoms to change their composition. It is a level of dominance that is absolute.

3e: Jesus created this earth

The Son of God formed this great world.

He created this earth!

Although man did not know he did.

Made long before his birth!

Jesus created this world:

> "He went and lived on Earth. And <u>even though he created it</u>, the world's inhabitants did not know who he was." **(Holy Bible: John 1:10)**

3f: Jesus created life

He breathed life into matter.

Structured life formed from clay!

He brought complexity from base.

In all of life's array!

As the Creator of all things, Jesus created life. This explains how the incredibly complex living cells can arise out of simple molecules even though abiogenesis is an impossible process within the prebiotic Earth's environment. A moving, growing watch that gives birth to other watches can never spontaneously arise out of a vat of simple molecules, regardless of the amount and duration of chemical reactions, since most complex molecules easily break apart at the slightest temperature or environmental change.

> "<u>He created the universe. Everything in heaven and earth, everything we see and cannot see,</u> including thrones, powers, rulers, or authorities; <u>he created them all</u>, and they are for him." (**Holy Bible: Colossians 1:16**)

3g: Jesus created humankind

> *Most of all, he created man.*
>
> *The pinnacle of life!*
>
> *Capable of moral reason.*
>
> *Can discern wrong from right!*

As the Creator of all things, Jesus created humanity:

> "To us, there is only one God, the Father, the originator of the universe and for whom we live; and there is one Lord Jesus Christ, the creator of the universe and <u>creator of humankind</u>." (**Holy Bible: 1 Corinthians 8:6**)

3h: We have free will

> *He gave us genuine freedom.*
>
> *We are free to obey him!*
>
> *He does not force us to be good.*
>
> *We must freely heed him!*

God does not manipulate or force us to be good and obey his will. We have genuine freedom. Christ knocks on our door—and we can either let him in, ignore him, or tell him to go away.

Moral discipline needs to be internal instead of external (imposed by the state or another authority figure).

> "<u>Christ has liberated us into freedom.</u> So, stand firm and do not allow yourself to get ensnared once more into the captivity of slavery. . .13 My brothers and sisters, <u>you have been called to be free</u>. Just do not use that freedom to indulge your fleshy urges but to lovingly serve one another. (**Holy Bible: Galatians 5:1,13**)

Clarification of the "4. Jesus Became Human" Stanzas

4a: Jesus became human flesh

The Creator became human.

Jesus Christ became flesh!

By becoming a mortal man.

He dignified our flesh!

The Bible repeatedly insists that Jesus *became* flesh, and everything that makes God "God" was in the physical body of Jesus Christ.

> *"<u>The Word became flesh</u> and lived among us. We have seen his glory—the glory of the only Son of the Father, full of grace and truth."* **(Holy Bible: John 1:14)**

> *"This is how you will know the Spirit of God: Every spirit that acknowledges <u>Jesus Christ came in the flesh</u> is of God! 3 Those who do not acknowledge Jesus are not from God. This is the spirit of the antichrist and is already in the world."* **(Holy Bible: 1 John 4:2-3)**

> *"There are many deceivers in the world who do not acknowledge <u>Jesus Christ came in the flesh</u>. These are deceivers and the antichrist."* **(Holy Bible: 2 John 1:7)**

> *"God was pleased that <u>all his fulness dwelt in Jesus</u>."* **(Holy Bible: Colossians 1:19)**

> *"<u>All of God's fulness dwells in the body of Jesus</u>."* **(Holy Bible: Colossians 2:9)**

The emphasis was on Jesus Christ becoming human "flesh" – the tangible matter that comprises our physical forms so that there can be no doubt that his incarnation was real.

When the Son of God became human, he, as a spirit entity, fused with every cell of his physical body. Each cell would have been energized with the "God" lifeforce so that there was no part of his body that was not united with his divine essence. In other words, all the fulness of God was in the physical body of Jesus Christ.

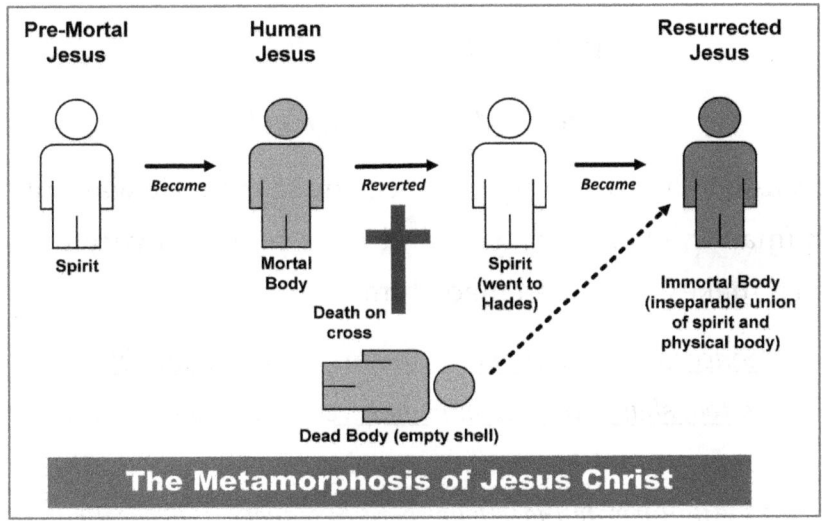

Jesus reverted to his prior spirit form when he died and then transformed into a glorified and immortal physical entity after his resurrection—one that could be physically felt, could eat and drink, and be discerned and communicated with by other humans. But this time, there can no longer be any separation of spirit and the material body. Jesus has an immortal physical body today and forevermore.

4b: Jesus became flesh to become a real human

He transformed from spirit to flesh.

He changed his state to mine!

Without this metamorphosis,

He couldn't save mankind!

Jesus was a spirit entity who became human. He was fully human in every way you and I are human. Everything that makes us human made him human.

> "<u>Since God's children are humans with flesh and blood, he, too, shared in that same nature</u> so that by his death, he may annul the devil, who holds the power of death, 15 And liberate those who were in slavery and terrified of death.
>
> 16 He did not come to help the angels; he came to help Abraham's descendants. 17 <u>This is why he needed to fully have the exact human nature as his siblings</u>, so that he may be a merciful and empathetic high priest before God, and offer an authentic sacrifice for the sins of humankind." **(Holy Bible: Hebrews 2:14-17)**

4c: Jesus became human to relate to humanity

He needed to relate to man.

He had to become man!

Jesus condemned sin in the flesh.

By becoming human!

Jesus becoming human flesh allowed him to share whatever we humans experience – our fear, pain, urges, and everything that makes us human. At the same time, he kept himself free from sin.

We sin and die thanks to our human flesh, but we are also made sinless and become immortal thanks to human flesh—Jesus Christ's.

"<u>Since God's children are humans with flesh and blood, he, too, shared in that same nature</u> so that by his death, he may annul the devil, who holds the power of death, 15 And liberate those who were in slavery and terrified of death.

16 He did not come to help the angels; he came to help Abraham's descendants. 17 <u>This is why he needed to fully have the exact human nature as his siblings, so that he may be a merciful and empathetic high priest before God, and offer an authentic sacrifice for the sins of humankind</u>.

> *18 <u>Because he knows what it is like to suffer when tempted, he can help those who are tempted.</u>"* **(Holy Bible: Hebrews 2:14-18)**

> *"<u>Since death came because of a man, it is necessary for the resurrection of the dead to also come from a man.</u>"* **(Holy Bible: 1 Corinthians 15:21)**

4d: Jesus bridged the God and human natures

> *Jesus bridged divine and human.*
>
> *He was both God and man!*
>
> *He was not half-God and half-man –*
>
> *He was full God and man!*

The Incarnation of Jesus Christ is a tremendously important detail since it means Jesus merged or fused within himself the two ontologically separate natures of God and Man.

> *"God did what the Law of Moses was incapable of doing due to the weakness of flesh: <u>God condemned sin in the flesh by sending his own Son to become flesh.</u>"* **(Holy Bible: Romans 8:3)**

Christ becoming human flesh makes his Incarnation, Atonement, and Resurrection real. It also means that the transformation of the Children of God after Judgment Day is similarly real and valid.

4e: Jesus humbled himself to become human

He humbled himself to be born.

The great God became man!

He emptied himself of glory.

From divine to mere man!

Jesus, the almighty Creator of the universe, is the ultimate example of humility:

"Have the same attitude Jesus Christ had:

6 <u>Although having the same nature as God, he did not think to forcefully cling to his equality with God,</u> 7 <u>but emptied himself of it, and took upon him the nature of a slave and became human</u>.

8 As a mortal man, <u>he humbled himself</u> and was so obedient to the Father's will that <u>he stooped to die the utterly degrading death on the cross</u>.

9 This is why God elevated him higher than anything possible and made his name more exalted than any other name.

10 And at the mention of Jesus's name, every knee in heaven, on earth, and in the underworld shall bend, 11 and everyone will concede that Jesus Christ is Lord, to the glory of God the Father." **(Holy Bible: Philippians 2:5-11)**

4f: Jesus was tempted but never sinned

He was tempted but never sinned.

Jesus never sinned!

He resisted all temptation.

Our Lord stayed free from sin!

Jesus stayed sinless throughout his life while being subject to the same urges and temptations we experience as humans.

> *"We do not have a high priest who is incapable of empathizing with our weaknesses. <u>He understands—he was also tempted in the same manner we are tempted—only he never sinned.</u>"* **(Holy Bible: Hebrews 4:15)**

4g: Jesus Christ can only have a single incarnation

He only becomes mortal once.

Just one mortality!

Death cannot again embrace him.

He rules death and Hades!

<u>**Jesus Christ can only become a mortal human *once*.**</u> He will never become mortal again and once more subject to sin and death.

> *There is no such thing as the repetitive mortality of the divine Christ, who manifests himself in different humans throughout history.*

The so-called divine "Christ" did not enter and then left the human "Jesus"; instead, the premortal "Only Begotten Son of God" <u>became</u> the human we know as "Jesus Christ":

> *"Know that <u>Christ</u> was resurrected from the dead—<u>he can never experience death again! Death can never again have power over him.</u> 10 <u>When he died, he died once for all time</u> to conquer sin. And the life he lives, he lives for God."* (**Holy Bible: Romans 6:9-10**)

> *"This is how you will know the Spirit of God: Every spirit that acknowledges <u>Jesus Christ came in the flesh</u> is of God! 3 Those who do not acknowledge Jesus are not from God. This is the spirit of the antichrist and is already in the world."* (**Holy Bible: 1 John 4:2-3**)

> *"There are many deceivers in the world who do not acknowledge <u>Jesus Christ came in the flesh</u>. These are deceivers and the antichrist."* (**Holy Bible: 2 John 1:7**)

So serious is this detail that John said that those who deny "Jesus Christ came in the flesh" are "antichrist" and are "deceivers."

The point of Christ's **Incarnation** was for the divine and human to unite completely, to create a bridge and conjoining that never existed before. All that makes God "God" was in Jesus Christ's flesh.

"God was pleased that <u>all his fulness dwelt in Jesus</u>." **(Holy Bible: Colossians 1:19)**

"<u>All of God's fulness dwells in the body of Jesus</u>." **(Holy Bible: Colossians 2:9)**

The point of Christ's **Atonement** was for the divine to assume the consequences of the sin and weakness of human flesh, to save those who have flesh from sin. And this sacrifice was only going to occur one time:

"It is God's will that we are purified and made spotless through the <u>one-time sacrifice</u> of the body of Jesus Christ.

11 Whereas every priest under the Law of Moses performed daily rituals and repeatedly offered the same sacrifices that could never remove sins. 12 But <u>Jesus offered one sacrifice for sins, once for all time</u>, and now sits on the right-hand side of God. 13 He is now just waiting for the appointed time when his enemies will be placed under his feet. 14 For <u>by one sacrifice, he has forever perfected those who are being purified and made spotless</u>." **(Holy Bible: Hebrews 10:10-14)**

The point of Christ's **Resurrection** was to destroy death and allow all who have ever lived as humans to live again with immortal physical bodies.

This means it is impossible for anyone to validly claim they are returning Jesus or Christ if they have a mortal body that can die, get sick, or feel pain. Those who do are false Christs.

The returning Jesus Christ will have a glorified immortal body incapable of feeling pain or getting killed. Punching him on the nose does nothing—he cannot feel pain, and no damage will ever occur. Stabbing him with a knife is like stabbing granite. Hitting him with a bat only breaks the bat and hurts your hand. Dunking his head under water will never cause him to drown. Poking him with a lit cigarette will never cause him to flinch or jump—and never burn his skin.

Also, the real returning Jesus Christ will come back in a manner visible to all, descending from the sky and accompanied by an enormous entourage—by his angels and his resurrected followers—after a global catastrophe.

Anyone who claims to be the returning Jesus or Christ should be willing to undergo simple tests to confirm he is who he claims to be. Bring a bat.

4h: Jesus was recognized by demons

The devils recognized Jesus.

They knew he was God's Son!

They begged him to let them be.

They feared God's only Son!

Recognition of Jesus Christ's true identity is not enough for salvation since even the demons recognized him:

> "<u>And demons also came out of many while shrieking:</u> <u>'You are the Son of God!'</u> He rebuked them and ordered them not to reveal his true identity because they knew he was the Messiah." **(Holy Bible: Luke 4:41)**

Clarification of the "5. The Atonement of Jesus" Stanzas

5a: Jesus Christ suffered

> Jesus suffered for mankind's sins.
>
> He took our punishments!
>
> God placed upon himself our sins,
>
> To save us from torments!

Christ's Atonement entailed real pain and suffering:

> "Jesus said, 'Father, if you are willing, please take this cup away from me. Nonetheless, let your will be done, not mine.' 43 An angel then appeared from heaven and encouraged him to go through with it.
>
> 44 <u>While being subjected to incomprehensible agony</u>, he prayed to the Father even more fervently, and <u>his sweat looked like blood and fell to the ground in clumps</u>." **(Holy Bible: Luke 22:42-44)**

HYMN STANZA CLARIFICATIONS | 163

"You were called for this purpose because Christ suffered for you. He is your example; follow his footsteps. 22 He never sinned and never deceived anyone. 23 When they vilified him, he did not retaliate. When <u>he suffered</u>, he did not make threats. He just relied upon God, who always judges justly. 24 <u>He bore our sins in his body on the cross so that we would die to sin but then live for righteousness. His wounds have healed you!</u>" **(1 Peter 2:21-24)**

5b: Jesus experienced an infinite Atonement

Christ's Atonement was infinite.

Pain, inconceivable!

It was infinite hurt and fear.

Unimaginable!

Christ's Atonement covers every human who has ever and will ever live due to the infinite worth of his blood as God incarnate:

"Jesus was temporarily made lower than angels. He is now crowned with glory and honor because he subjected himself to death. By God's grace, <u>he died for everyone</u>! 10 It was appropriate that he who inherited the universe and created it, and who brings many children to glory as the source of their salvation, would become perfect through his suffering." **(Holy Bible: Hebrews 2:9-10)**

> *"They sought to know the time and circumstance the Spirit of Christ was alluding to when he told them in advance that <u>the Messiah would suffer</u>, and the great glory afterward...*
>
> *18 As you know, gold and silver were not used to pay your ransom from the futile life you received from your ancestors, 19 but with the <u>incalculably valuable</u> blood of Christ, the unblemished and spotless Lamb of God, 20 who was chosen before the world was created, and was revealed in these last days for your sake."* (**Holy Bible: 1 Peter 1:11,18-20**)

5c: Jesus was a sinless substitute

> *He was a sinless substitute.*
>
> *He was the Lamb of God!*
>
> *He was a stain-free sacrifice.*
>
> *An offering to God!*

Jesus was our sinless substitute, who took upon himself the punishments for our sins:

> *"God showed his love toward us by sending his only Son into the world so that we might live through him. 10 This is real love: Not that we loved God, but because he loved us—and <u>sent his Son to be the appeasing sacrifice for our sins</u>! . . . 14 And we have seen and testify that*

the Father sent his Son to be the Savior of humankind."
(Holy Bible: 1 John 4:9-10,14)

5d: Jesus paid our ransom and freed us

Jesus ransomed himself for us.

Because of him, we're free!

Christ's holy blood paid the ransom.

We slaves can now be free!

Christ paid our ransom by substituting himself and setting us free from bondage:

"He gave himself as a ransom for all, and is witnessed to all the world at the right time." **(Holy Bible: 1 Timothy 2:6)**

5e: Jesus died for humankind

Jesus died for humanity.

He died for you and me!

God's only Son died for our sins.

Despite we're not worthy!

Christ died for all of humankind:

"For while we were powerless, Christ died at the appointed time for us sinners. 7 It is rare for someone to give up his life for a righteous person except, perhaps, for an especially good man. 8 But God proved his great

love for us—<u>although we were sinners, Christ died for us</u>!" **(Holy Bible: Romans 5:6-8)**

5f: Jesus's sacrifice/blood reconciles us to God

He reconciles us to our God.

His blood justifies us!

His sacrifice reconciles us.

His blood sanctifies us!

Christ's sacrifice reconciles us to God:

"And <u>through Jesus, God reconciled the universe to himself, whether things on earth or in the heavens—by making peace through Jesus's blood on the cross</u>. 21 You were once alienated from God, with a hostile mind because of your evil actions. 22 But now, <u>Jesus has reconciled you in his flesh through his death, to present you to God, holy, unblemished, and beyond reproach</u>." **(Holy Bible: Colossians 1:20-22)**

5g: Jesus's blood forgives sins

We're redeemed through his holy blood.

We're washed clean in his blood!

His shed blood removes mankind's sins.

Made sinless through his blood!

Christ's blood forgives our sins:

> "But if we walk in the light, as he is in the light, we participate with one another, and <u>the blood of his Son, Jesus, cleanses us from all sin.</u>" **(Holy Bible: 1 John 1:7)**

5h: We participate with Jesus Christ

> *We are nailed to the cross with him.*
>
> *We're crucified with Christ!*
>
> *We share his death; we share his rise.*
>
> *We live to God in Christ!*

Christ's true follower participates in his death and resurrection. Somehow, Christ's Incarnation into human flesh allows us to become one with Christ's death and resurrection so that the effects of those actions apply to us:

> *"Do you not know that <u>we who are baptized into Jesus Christ are baptized into his death</u>? 4 <u>We were buried with him by baptism into death.</u> And <u>just as Christ rose from the dead by the Father's glory, so, too, we rise and live a new life.</u> 5 <u>Since we are united with him in his death, so, too, will we be united in his resurrection.</u>*
>
> *6 We know that <u>our old self was crucified with him</u> so that the body of sin will be annulled and free us from slavery to sin, 7 because those who are dead have been*

*freed from sin. 8 If we died with Christ, we also believe that we will live with him." (**Holy Bible: Romans 6:3-8**)*

*"Here is a saying we can trust: 'If we die together with him, we will live together with him!'" (**Holy Bible: 2 Timothy 2:11**)*

Clarification of the "6. The Resurrection of Jesus" Stanzas

6a: Jesus preached to the spirits in prison

Meeting the spirits in prison,

Jesus preached to the dead!

The Son of God fulfilled his task –

His suffering ended!

Where did Jesus go, and what did he do during the three days between his death and resurrection?

He preached to the dead:

"Because Christ suffered a single time for sins, the righteous for the unrighteous, to bring you to God. He was put to death in the body but made alive in the Spirit. 19 He then went and preached to the spirits in prison, 20 who were disobedient from long ago, when God waited patiently while Noah was building an ark, so

that a few, just eight people, were saved through water."
(Holy Bible: 1 Peter 3:18-20)

The gospel is preached not just to the living but also to the dead (1 Peter 4:6) who are currently in Hades. This heaven/hell or paradise/prison is where all humans go upon death as disembodied spirits until we are all resurrected into immortal, physical bodies to stand and be judged by Jesus Christ before the Father at Judgment Day.

6b: Angels announced Jesus's resurrection

Angels proclaimed glorious news:

Jesus came back from death!

He is not here; he is risen.

He once again has breath!

Christ's Atonement was the most significant event in the history of the universe. That pivotal moment sealed the fate of the universe, humanity, all life, and Satan and his demons.

Christ's resurrection was the conclusion of the Atonement and destroyed death's control over us. His rising from the dead showed the futility of Satan's rebellion. That empty tomb proved that he completed what the Father asked and is now just waiting for the appointed time to receive his inheritance and recognition.

There is now *no* risk that God's plan can be thwarted by Jesus failing in his task.

> *"But when they entered the tomb, they did not find the body of the Lord Jesus. 4 While they stood there confused, suddenly, two men wearing dazzling robes appeared in their midst!*
>
> *5 Terrified, the women prostrated themselves before the men, who then told them, 'Why are you looking among the dead for someone alive? 6 <u>He is not here—he is risen from the dead!</u> Remember when he told you back in Galilee, 7 that the Son of Man needs to be handed over to sinful men to be crucified to death only to rise again after three days?'*
>
> *8 Then the women remembered Jesus told them these things were going to happen."* (**Holy Bible: Luke 24:3-8**)

6c: Jesus rose from the dead

>*Jesus Christ was resurrected.*
>
>*Jesus conquered the grave!*
>
>*Returning from the realm of death,*
>
>*Never again death's slave!*

The most fantastic news imaginable: Jesus Christ came back to life after being dead for three days!

"Remember <u>Jesus Christ</u>, the descendant of David, <u>was raised from the dead</u>! This is the good news I am preaching!" (**Holy Bible: 2 Timothy 2:8**)

6d: Many eyewitnesses saw, interacted with, and touched the resurrected Jesus

He spent time with his disciples.

His body could be felt!

Forty days they walked together,

Then rising up to dwelt!

Over 500 eyewitnesses saw Jesus after his resurrection (1 Corinthians 15:6), and their testimony was the foundation of the early church's credibility. Christ's resurrection was a physical one – his followers could feel his body with their hands. It was a "spiritual" body because it was no longer subject to the mortal body's vulnerabilities (he could not get killed again or feel pain or discomfort of any kind). Still, there is no doubt it was a material resurrected body.

"As they hastily left the tomb with fear and great joy, and were rushing to tell the disciples what the angel instructed, 9 Jesus met them and said, "Greetings!" They then prostrated themselves before him and <u>held on to his feet</u>, and worshiped him." (**Holy Bible: Matthew 28:8-9**)

"While they were talking about these things, Jesus suddenly appeared in their midst and said, 'May you have peace.' 37 They then jumped in terror and feared they saw a ghost. 38 He said to them, 'Why are you frightened? Why are your hearts filled with doubt? 39 <u>Look at my hands and my feet. It is me! Touch me and confirm it is me. A ghost does not have a body of flesh and bone that you see I have.</u>'

40 He then showed them his hands and feet, 41 and while they still could not believe it was him out of sheer joy and amazement, he asked them, <u>'Do you have anything to eat?' 42 They then handed him some broiled fish, 43 which he then ate in front of them</u>.

44 He then said, 'This is what I told you before—everything about me that is written in the law of Moses, the prophets, and psalms need to be fulfilled.' 45 He then opened their minds so that they could completely understand the scriptures, 46 and told them, 'This is what was written: The Messiah needs to suffer and rise from the dead after three days. 47 Repentance and forgiveness of sins are proclaimed in his name, starting in Jerusalem. 48 You are witnesses of these things. 49 And now, I am going to send to you what my Father has promised. So, stay in the city until the power from heaven clothes you.'

50 He led them close to Bethany when he then raised his hands toward heaven and blessed them. 51 While he was blessing them, he started rising up into the air and was then carried off into heaven." (**Holy Bible: Luke 24:36-51**)

6e: Jesus was first to resurrect from the dead as an immortal body

>*He's first to be resurrected.*
>
>*The first immortal flesh!*
>
>*Our Lord's the firstborn from the dead.*
>
>*Praise him who conquered death!*

While the Bible describes cases of people coming back to life before Christ's resurrection (such as those brought back to life by Elijah and Elisha, the Nain widow's son, the daughter of Jairus, and Lazarus), Christ's resurrection was different because he was the first to be resurrected as an *immortal* body. All others who were brought back to life were still mortal – at some point, they died again.

>*"In reality, <u>Christ truly rose from the dead and was the very first person to ever come back to life after dying</u>. . . 23 But each according to their place in line: <u>Christ is the first to live again</u>, followed by those who belong to him when he returns."* (**Holy Bible: 1 Corinthians 15:20,23**)

6f: Jesus will destroy death and Hades

Christ will forever destroy death.

I no longer fear death!

Christ holds the keys of death and Hades.

Jesus will annul death!

Jesus was dead but came back to life. In so doing, he possesses the "keys" of death and the realm of the dead and controls who comes in and goes out. After death and hell are "emptied," they will be destroyed, never again to contain deceased humans – since there will never again be any dead humans.

"I am the living one. <u>I was dead but look at me now—I am alive and will be for all eternity. I hold the keys of Death and Hades</u>." **(Holy Bible: Revelation 1:18)**

"<u>The last enemy he will annul is death</u>." **(Holy Bible: 1 Corinthians 15:26)**

"The sea gave up the dead who were in it, and Death and Hades gave up the dead that were in them—and each person was judged according to what they did. 14 <u>Then Death and Hades were thrown into the lake of fire</u>. The second death is the lake of fire." **(Holy Bible: Revelation 20:13-14)**

6g: Jesus can never die again

Jesus can never die again.

Just one mortality!

Death can never again have him.

He lives eternally!

Jesus can never experience death again, which means he can never become a mortal human that is once more subject to pain and death:

> "Know that <u>Christ was resurrected from the dead—he can never experience death again! Death can never again have power over him</u>. 10 When he died, he died once for all time to conquer sin. And the life he lives, he lives for God." **(Holy Bible: Romans 6:9-10)**

6h: Jesus makes everyone immortal

Christ makes everyone immortal –

Both righteous and flawed!

This bequest he gives to us all.

In our flesh, we'll see God!

Jesus Christ's resurrection gives all humans a gift, regardless of their righteousness and belief in him or lack thereof. He will make all humans immortal, with physical, material bodies that can never die:

"_In Adam, everyone dies; in Christ, everyone will live again._" (**Holy Bible: 1 Corinthians 15:22**)

"_Do not be so surprised because the time is coming when all those who are dead will hear his voice, 29 and will come out of the grave. Those who have lived righteously will receive a resurrection of life, while those who have been evil will receive a resurrection where they will be condemned._" (**Holy Bible: John 5:28-29**)

"_I have the same hope in God that these men have — that there will be a resurrection of both the righteous and unrighteous._" (**Holy Bible: Acts 24:15**)

Clarification of the "7. The Glorification of Jesus" Stanzas

7a: Jesus is glorified and exalted above all

The Father glorifies his Son.

He has God's own glory!

Christ is exalted above all.

Because he was worthy!

The Father glorifies his triumphant Son – Jesus did what no other entity could do: perform an infinite Atonement. In doing so, he reconciled us to God and freed us from our slavery to sin and death.

"Jesus was temporarily made lower than angels. <u>He is now crowned with glory and honor because he subjected himself to death</u>. By God's grace, he died for everyone!" **(Holy Bible: Hebrews 2:9)**

*"This is why <u>God elevated him higher than anything possible and made his name more exalted than any other name</u>." ***(Holy Bible: Philippians 2:9)**

7b: Jesus's name is above all names/he is Lord

His name is above all names.

Jesus is over all!

All will concede Jesus is Lord.

Jesus is Lord of all!

Jesus Christ's actions of becoming human flesh, paying our ransom by his suffering and death, and coming back from the dead (the Incarnation, Atonement, and Resurrection) are so enormous, so vital, and so integral to our ultimate fate and happiness that every one of us, will acknowledge our debt and gratitude toward him.

"This is why <u>God elevated him higher than anything possible and made his name more exalted than any other name</u>. 10 And <u>at the mention of Jesus's name, every knee in heaven, on earth, and in the underworld shall bend</u>, 11 and <u>everyone will concede that Jesus Christ is

<u>Lord</u>, to the glory of God the Father." **(Holy Bible: Philippians 2:9-11)**

Even those who will be eternally condemned due to their evil works will still concede in gratitude that Jesus Christ is Lord because they will not remain disembodied spirits, but will be resurrected with immortal bodies thanks to Christ's gift to all of material immortality.

7c: Jesus is exalted to God's right-hand side

Exalted to the Father's right.

Our Lord's at God's right hand!

Seat of honor, might, and glory –

Before of which we'll stand!

Jesus is now on the Father's right-hand side to rule over all beneath the Father's authority.

> "Similarly, baptism also saves you. Not by the washing away of dirt from your bodies, but as an appeal to God to give you a clear conscience through the resurrection of <u>Jesus Christ</u> – 22 <u>Who is ascended into heaven and sits on God's right-hand side. All angels, authorities, and powers are made subject to him</u>." **(Holy Bible: 1 Peter 3:21-22)**

HYMN STANZA CLARIFICATIONS | 179

7d: Jesus is the only way to God/he is the only way for us to be saved

Jesus is the only way to God.

He stands before God's throne!

No one can receive salvation –

Lest going through God's Son!

The world does not want to hear it, but there is no ambiguity. There are not many ways to heaven. There is only one way: Through Jesus Christ.

"Jesus said to them, 'I am the Way, and the Truth, and the Life. No one can come unto the Father except through me.'" **(Holy Bible: John 14:6)**

"Know this, you people of Israel, that this man was healed due to the name of Jesus Christ of Nazareth, whom you crucified, but whom God raised from the dead.

11 Jesus is the stone that the builders rejected that is now the cornerstone. 12 Salvation cannot be found in anyone else! There is no other name given to humankind that can save us!" **(Holy Bible: Acts 4:10-12)**

It does not matter if this message is offensive. It is irrelevant if it is not politically correct. It is immaterial if popular culture, the media, politicians, the government, or other religions punish those who unapologetically say this out loud. All will know this truth when we die and stand to be judged: Jesus Christ is the only way for us to be saved.

7e: Jesus receives the universe as an inheritance and reigns over it

> *God gave his Son the universe.*
>
> *Dominion over all!*
>
> *An eternal inheritance.*
>
> *Beneath his feet are all!*

This inconceivably vast universe belongs to Christ as an inheritance from Heavenly Father.

> *"And now, God has spoken to us through his Son in these last days. <u>God has given the universe to him as an inheritance</u>, and created it through him." (**Holy Bible: Hebrews 1:2**)*

> *"<u>The Father loves the Son and has given him the universe</u>." (**Holy Bible: John 3:35**)*

> *"<u>Jesus knew that the Father gave him dominion over the entire universe</u> and that he came from God and will return to God." (**Holy Bible: John 13:3**)*

7f: Jesus will return to earth with great power and glory

Jesus Christ will return to earth.

He will come suddenly!

With angels and the righteous dead.

With great might and glory!

When Jesus returns to Earth, he will approach the planet from space and be accompanied by a throng of angels. All the inhabitants of Earth will see his coming. As he gets closer, his righteous followers who are dead will be resurrected and float up to join his group while he is still above the Earth. After this occurs, his followers who are still mortal will abruptly become immortal, where their mortal bodies change to glorified ones, and they, too, will ascend to meet the returning Christ. He will then descend and touch the Earth's surface with his feet and usher in the end of the age.

*"And then the sign of the Son of Man will appear in heaven. And then <u>all nations shall mourn and will see the Son of Man arrive on the clouds, with great power and glory</u>." (**Holy Bible: Matthew 24:30**)*

*"To you who are being oppressed, rest assured that you will find relief together with us when <u>the Lord Jesus appears from heaven with his mighty angels</u>." (**Holy Bible: 2 Thessalonians 1:7**)*

"For if we believe that Jesus died and rose again, we also believe that <u>when Jesus returns, God will have those who have died having faith in Jesus, accompany him</u>. 15 We tell you this directly from the Lord: His followers who will still be alive when the Lord comes will not precede those who have already died. 16 For <u>the Lord himself will descend from heaven and will command</u>, using the voice of an archangel and a blaring trumpet, <u>for his dead followers to rise and meet him first</u>. 17 <u>After this happens, those of us who are still alive will rise into the air to meet the Lord among the clouds</u>, and we will be with the Lord forever." **(Holy Bible: 2 Thessalonians 4:14-17)**

7g: Jesus will resurrect and judge humankind

Jesus will resurrect us all;

Both the good and the bad!

He will judge all men and women –

To be saved or condemned!

The scriptures describe Jesus Christ's resurrection as a complete triumph over death itself. He gives a gift to all humanity—the gift of immortality—where all humans will receive immortal, perfected physical bodies, irrespective of their belief or unbelief in him and regardless of their good or evil works. These "spiritual" bodies are somewhat identical to his resurrected body, which could be touched, can eat and drink, and so forth.

A "spiritual" body means a <u>physical,</u> material body that is not subject to death and harm and can do things normal mortal bodies cannot do. It is not something immaterial or insubstantial (which would negate the whole point of Christ's resurrection and triumph over "death").

After we resurrect as immortal physical bodies, we will all stand before God and be judged by Jesus Christ:

"Do not be so surprised because the time is coming when <u>all those who are dead will hear his voice,</u> 29 <u>and will come out of the grave. Those who have lived righteously will receive a resurrection of life while those who have been evil will receive a resurrection where they will be condemned."</u> **(Holy Bible: John 5:28-29)**

"I have the same hope in God that these men have—that <u>there will be a resurrection of both the righteous and unrighteous.</u>" **(Holy Bible: Acts 24:15)**

"If it is being preached that Christ rose from the dead, how is it possible some of you are claiming there is no such thing as the resurrection of the dead? 13 But <u>if there is no resurrection of the dead, then Christ did not rise from the dead either.</u> 14 And if Christ did not rise, then our preaching is pointless, and your faith is

pointless as well. 15 Not just that, but we would also be exposed as liars because we had testified that God raised up Christ when, in fact, he did not—if the dead are not resurrected. 16 <u>For if the dead are not resurrected, neither has Christ been resurrected.</u> 17 And if Christ has not been raised from the dead, then your faith is pointless, and you are still in your sins. 18 Furthermore, those who have already died while having faith in Christ are irretrievably gone. 19 If only in this life can we have hope in Christ, we are pitiful.

20 In reality, Christ truly rose from the dead and was the very first person to ever come back to life after dying. 21 Since death came because of a man, it is necessary for the resurrection of the dead to also come from a man.

22 In Adam, everyone dies; <u>in Christ, everyone will live again</u>. 23 But each according to their place in line: <u>Christ is the first to live again, followed by those who belong to him when he returns.</u>

24 Then the end will come when he hands over the kingdom to God the Father (after he annuls all rulers, authorities, and powers). 25 He must reign until he puts all his enemies under his feet.

26 <u>The last enemy he will annul is death</u>. 27 For he has dominion over all things. However, when it says, "All things," it is evident that that excludes God, who gave Jesus dominion over the universe. 28 After all things are put under the Son's authority, he then is placed under the Father's authority so that God may have dominion over all.

29 Finally, if there is no resurrection, why are those who are baptized for the dead doing it? <u>If the dead are not going to rise, why then are they baptized for them?</u> 30 And why are we in constant danger from others?" **(Holy Bible: 1 Corinthians 15:12-30)**

"For the Son of Man will come in his Father's glory, and his angels shall accompany him. <u>He will then judge all humans according to their works.</u>" **(Holy Bible: Matthew 16:27)**

"<u>We must all stand before the judgment-seat of Christ so that each of us will be judged based on what we have done in our lives, whether good or bad.</u>" **(Holy Bible: 2 Corinthians 5:10)**

7h: Jesus will replace heaven and earth

He will replace heaven and earth.

A new heaven and earth!

The old versions obsoleted;

The new: No sin, no death!

Regardless of our attachment to material things, this Earth will not last in its present state. Just as humans are going to be changed from mortal to immortal; so, too, will the Earth:

> "And <u>I saw a new earth and sky, for the earlier earth and sky had disappeared</u>, and the sea disappeared as well." **(Holy Bible: Revelation 21:1)**

> "The day of the Lord will come unexpectedly, like a thief in the night. <u>The sky will disappear with a terrible roar, and the Earth's materials will burn away</u>, exposing all its secrets and evil deeds.

> 11 Since these things are going to disappear, what type of person should you then be? You should be righteous and godly, 12 <u>looking forward to the day of God, and pushing for it to come sooner, where the sky burns, and the Earth's materials melt from the heat.</u> 13 <u>This is so that his promise of a new heaven and new earth will finally occur, where only righteousness dwells."</u> **(Holy Bible: 2 Peter 3:10-13)**

> "All of creation eagerly waits in anticipation for God to reveal who his Children are!

> 20 Creation became corrupt, not through its own fault, but because God subjected it in the hope 21 that <u>after creation is freed from its bondage to decay, it will share in the freedom of the glory of the Children of God</u>." **(Holy Bible: Romans 8:19-21)**

Clarification of the "8. Jesus Creates the Children of God" Stanzas

8a: Belief in Jesus brings eternal life

Follow Christ for eternal life.

Believe him and be saved!

He's the living bread from heaven.

Have faith, repent, be kind!

Those who believe in Jesus Christ and strive to follow him will be rewarded with "eternal life." This is different from becoming immortal:

- Immortality – Having a perfected physical body that can never die or be subject to discomfort, damage, or pain

- Eternal Life – Living with God for all eternity in a state of happiness

Christ's followers receive both rewards while the wicked and those who reject him only receive immortality.

> "So that whoever believes in him shall not perish but have eternal life. 16 God loved humankind so much that he gave up his only Son. Whoever believes in him shall not perish but have eternal life. . . 36 Whoever believes in the Son has eternal life. On the other hand, whoever

does not obey him will never experience eternal life, and God's wrath remains on him." **(Holy Bible: John 3:15-16,36)**

8b: We must obey Jesus

We are to keep his commandments.

Believe him and obey!

Do good and show love and mercy.

Love all, and always pray!

The condition for true discipleship is obedience to Jesus Christ's commands. Since none of us can obey perfectly, we must then <u>strive</u> to obey, repent when (not if, when) we fail, make restitution when we can, but always have faith in him and continually make an effort to improve and obey.

"<u>If you keep my commandments, you will stay in my love</u>, even as I keep my Father's commandments and stay within his love." **(Holy Bible: John 15:10)**

"And being perfected, <u>he became the source of eternal salvation for all who obey him</u>." **(Holy Bible: Hebrews 5:9)**

"But is now revealed, and by the prophetic scriptures according to the everlasting God's command <u>so that all nations will know the obedience that comes from faith</u>." **(Holy Bible: Romans 16:26)**

8c: Jesus enables his followers to be adopted by his Father

God adopts us because of Christ.

We can be born of God!

The Lord's foster sons and daughters.

By grace, Children of God!

Christ enables his faithful followers to be adopted by God:

"You have received a Spirit that does not enslave you and makes you afraid once more. <u>You have received a Spirit of divine adoption as sons and daughters. We can now call him, 'Abba! Father!'</u> . . . 22 We know that all of creation has been continually groaning as if it is experiencing the pain of childbirth. 23 Not just creation—although we have received the first portions of the Spirit, <u>we are also groaning while we eagerly wait for our adoption as sons and daughters</u>, and the redemption of our bodies." (**Holy Bible: Romans 8:15,22-23**)

"<u>You are the Sons and Daughters of God through faith in Christ Jesus</u>. 27 All of you who have been baptized into Christ have become enveloped by Christ. 28 There is no Jew or Gentile, slave or free, or male or female: You are all one in Christ Jesus. 29 And if you are Christ's,

then you are Abraham's descendants and heirs of the divine promise.

4:1 What I am saying is that as long as the heir is still a child, it is as if he is a slave despite actually owning the estate. 2 He is still under the authority of his guardians and trustees until reaching the age his father set for him.

3 Similarly, while we were still children, we were enslaved under the control of the world's principles, 4 but when the appointed time arrived, <u>God sent his Son</u>, born of a woman, born under the law, 5 <u>to redeem those enslaved to the Law and adopt us as his Sons and Daughters</u>.

6 <u>Because you are Sons and Daughters, God sent the Spirit of his Son into our hearts so that we may be able to cry out loud: 'Abba! Father!'</u> 7 <u>As a result, you are no longer a slave, but a Son or Daughter; and if so, then an heir of God</u>." **(Holy Bible: Galatians 3:26-4:7)**

"Just as God chose us to be within Jesus since before the world was created (for us to be holy and blameless within 'love' when we are in front of God), 5 <u>we were predestined to be divinely adopted as God's children through Jesus Christ</u>, in accordance with his pleasure and desire." **(Holy Bible: Ephesians 1:4-5)**

8d: Jesus's true followers become the Children of God and God's heirs

> *The Children of God are his heirs.*
>
> *By grace, we are his heirs!*
>
> *No longer specks, but now his heirs.*
>
> *With Jesus, fellow-heirs!*

Christ's true followers become the exalted "Children of God" and his "Heirs":

> *"If you know that he is righteous, you then know that <u>all who do righteousness are his children</u>.*
>
> *3:1 See how much the Father loves us: <u>We shall be called the "Children of God," which is precisely what we are!</u> Because of this, the world does not recognize us because it does not know him.*
>
> *2 Dear friends, <u>we are already the Children of God, but he has not yet revealed to us what exactly we will be, only that when Jesus appears, we will become like him, for we will see him as he truly is</u>, 3 and all who have this hope within them purify themselves, even as Jesus is pure."* **(Holy Bible: 1 John 2:29-3:3)**
>
> *"For <u>those whom the Spirit of God leads are the Children of God</u>. 15 You have received a Spirit that does not enslave you and makes you afraid once more. You*

have received a Spirit of divine adoption as sons and daughters. We can now call him, 'Abba! Father!'

16 The Spirit himself testifies with our spirit that we are the Children of God. 17 <u>If we are children, then we are heirs—heirs of God and fellow-heirs with Christ, provided we suffer with him so that we may be glorified together.</u> 18 I do not consider our current sufferings to be anywhere comparable to the coming glory that will be revealed to us.

19 <u>All of creation eagerly waits in anticipation for God to reveal who his Children are!</u>

20 Creation became corrupt, not through its own fault, but because God subjected it in the hope 21 that after creation is freed from its bondage to decay, it will share in the freedom of the glory of the Children of God." **(Holy Bible: Romans 8:14-21)**

"<u>They who overcome will inherit these things. I will be their God, and they will be my son or daughter.</u>" **(Holy Bible: Revelation 21:7)**

8e: The Children of God share oneness and mutual indwelling with God

God's children share oneness with him.

Dwelling in each other!

We live in them; they live in us.

None without the other!

The "Children of God" will share oneness and mutual indwelling with God:

"'On that day, you will understand that I am in my Father, and <u>you are in me, and I am in you</u>.' . . . 23 Jesus replied, 'Those who love me will keep my teachings, and my Father will love them. We will come to them and <u>will dwell within them</u>.'" (**Holy Bible: John 14:20,23**)

"Holy Father, I am about to leave this world and go to you, but they are staying in this world. Protect them by the power of your name <u>so that they may be one as we are one</u>. . . 21 <u>That they may be one just as you are in me and I in you</u>. <u>May they be in us</u> so that the world may believe that you sent me. 22 I gave them the glory you gave <u>me so that they may be one just as we are one</u>. 23 <u>I in them and you in me,</u> so that they may become perfectly united. The world will then know that you sent me and loved them just as you loved me." (**Holy Bible: John 17:11,21-23**)

> "*<u>Whoever is joined to the Lord is one spirit</u>.*" **(Holy Bible: 1 Corinthians 6:17)**

8f: The Children of God share the divine nature

> *Sharing in the divine nature,*
>
> *God shares himself with us!*
>
> *Transforming to Christ's same image,*
>
> *Awaits his followers!*

The Children of God share in the divine nature, the very nature of God:

> *"His divine power has given us all things relating to life and godliness through the knowledge of the one who called us by his own glory and virtue, 4 through which he has given us precious and magnificent promises: After we have escaped from the corruption of the sinful desires of the world, <u>we can share in the divine nature</u>!"* **(Holy Bible: 2 Peter 1:3-4)**

> *"The veil has been removed from our face, and we can see the glory of the Lord reflected in a mirror. Thanks to the Lord's Spirit, <u>we are undergoing metamorphosis into the same image</u>."* **(Holy Bible: 2 Corinthians 3:18)**

> *"Until we achieve the unity of the faith and knowledge of the Son of God, and grow <u>up until finally measuring up to the dimensions of the fullness of Christ's nature</u>. .*

. 15 Rather, we speak the truth in love: We should grow up into him in all things, who is the head, Christ. . . 24 And to <u>put on the new nature, which is after God's</u>, created in righteousness and holy truth." (**Holy Bible: Ephesians 4:13,15,24**)

8g: The Children of God share God's glory

Christ shares glory with God's children.

God's heirs share in glory!

Christ gives us his glory from God.

His heirs receive glory!

The Children of God receive incredible glory – and share in the glory of God:

"<u>I gave them the glory you gave me</u> so that they may be one just as we are one." (**Holy Bible: John 17:22**)

"Through whom we have access to this grace we are currently standing in because of our faith, <u>and we boast of our hope in sharing the glory of God.</u>" (**Holy Bible: Romans 5:2**)

"If we are children, then we are heirs—heirs of God and fellow-heirs with Christ, provided we suffer with <u>him so that we may be glorified together.</u>" (**Holy Bible: Romans 8:17**)

"Our troubles are minor and momentary—but will result <u>in us obtaining an incredible glory that lasts forever!</u>" (**Holy Bible: 2 Corinthians 4:17**)

8h: The Children of God share rule and everything Jesus has

Jesus shares all he has with us –

For those who stay faithful!

Those who endure will rule with him –

A gift so wonderful!

Jesus shares everything he has with the Children of God. This includes sharing rule over the universe since he received it as an inheritance from the Father:

"<u>We have become entitled to share everything Christ has – if we keep our initial belief by staying faithful until the end.</u>" (**Holy Bible: Hebrews 3:14**)

"<u>If we endure, we will reign together with him</u>; if we deny him, he will deny us." (**Holy Bible: 2 Timothy 2:12**)

"<u>I will give those who overcome the right to sit with me on my throne</u>—just as I overcame and sat down with my Father on his throne." (**Holy Bible: Revelation 3:21**)

"<u>He has made us kings and priests for God, his Father</u>. To him be glory and dominion forevermore! Amen." **(Holy Bible: Revelation 1:6)**

"Even while dead in sin, we came back to life together with Christ (you are saved by grace) 6 and rose up together, and <u>are to be seated together in the heavenly realms in unity with Christ Jesus,</u> 7 <u>so that God may show all future ages how incalculably rich his grace is</u> because of his kindness toward us in Christ Jesus." **(Holy Bible: Ephesians 2:5-7)**

Jesus shares the stupendous gift of ruling over the universe with those who will become the glorified "Children of God." This is so enormous and so magnificent that it will be everlasting evidence to all creatures in the universe of just how "incalculably rich his grace is."

CONCLUSION

There is no doubt that Jesus Christ is the most influential person in history. So colossal is his impact that every person today has tangibly benefited from his teachings and influence. He is the outlier of outliers. Furthermore, if the Holy Bible is to be believed, then he created the universe and became human two millennia ago. He performed the infinite Atonement whereby we can be saved and even become the immortal rulers of the universe beneath his dominion as his "fellow-heirs" if we faithfully follow him.

The Holy Bible contains evidence of its credibility within itself – *the New Testament is a frameless, unharmonized, correlative anthology.* This is such a powerful witness that when I saw its single coherent cosmology, I instantly lost my atheism and regained my faith in Jesus Christ. This is because it is demonstrably impossible for nine people to write books whose contents blend to create a single picture without using a common frame (such as author guidelines) or having their deliverables harmonized by a joint editor.

My decades of experience analyzing complex documentation confirms to me that the empirical evidence for the New Testament is credible and likely. This validation provides intellectual support to the much more critical subjective witness from the Holy Spirit telling me that Jesus is truly God made flesh who suffered and died for our sakes so that we may become one with him and his Father and share in their very nature.

Reading the Part 2 hymns comforts me, and I feel the Holy Spirit confirming that the phrasings accurately depict our Lord and Savior and issues relating to him.

I am so grateful for regaining my faith in Christ in 2016 and for not dying as an atheist while willfully disobeying his will.

I am humbled by the gift of repentance! I recognize that the opportunity to repent is a blessing beyond imagination, and I seized it with both hands. My soul is now at peace, and I strive to love God, my neighbor, myself, and keep God's commandments. And while I am constantly failing and sinning, I am continually repenting and endeavoring to be better.

I look forward to that day when I stand before my God and tell him how much I love him and am grateful for what he did for us.

While I want to become one of the Children of God – one of those whom God will adopt to share in his divine nature, oneness, and mutual indwelling, I do not demand it. Only Christ, the great Judge, decides my fate. All I know for sure is whatever judgment Christ imposes on me will be just and exactly what I deserve.

Becoming the adopted Son or Daughter of God is such an overwhelming gift that it is impossible to grasp that adoption's significance.

Here we are, mere specks, but subject to a divine promise that can only be fulfilled by obedience to the Son of God.

So, my brothers and sisters, let us follow him wherever he leads us and endure to the end. In so doing, we live a life of meaning and joy regardless of what others do to us and eternal life in the next.

In the name of Jesus Christ, my Savior and God. Amen.

SCRIPTURE REFERENCE GUIDE

Old Testament

Genesis
Gen 2:4 .... 126, 130

Exodus
Ex 3:14 .... 58, 126
Ex 13:21-22 128

Deuteronomy
Deut 6:16 129
Deut 10:17 127
Deut 32:3-4 128
Deut 32:39 .... 58, 126
Deut 32:43 130
Deut 33:2 129

2 Kings
2 Kg 17:13 127

1 Chronicles
1 Chr 16:33 127

2 Chronicles
2 Chr 36:15-16 127

Nehemiah
Neh 9:6 129

Job
Job 4:9 128
Job 9:8 129
Job 38:1-4 .... 126, 130

Psalms
Ps 8:1-3 .... 126, 130
Ps 9:7 127
Ps 22 138
Ps 23:1 127
Ps 31:5 130
Ps 31:20 128
Ps 32:7 128
Ps 45:6-7 130
Ps 47:5 129
Ps 50:6 127
Ps 57:1 128
Ps 62:6-7 128
Ps 65:5-8 129
Ps 91:1-10 128
Ps 96:13 127
Ps 97:7 130
Ps 99:6 128

Ps 102:24-27 130
Ps 102:25 .... 126, 130
Ps 116:13,17 128
Ps 118:22 128
Ps 136:3 127
Ps 148:5-6 129

Isaiah

Isa 2:12 129
Isa 6:1-10 127
Isa 8:13-14 128
Isa 9:6 119
Isa 11:4 128
Isa 12:4 128
Isa 31:5 128
Isa 40:3-9 127
Isa 41:4 .... 58, 126
Isa 43:10 .... 58, 126
Isa 43:11 .... 58, 126
Isa 43:14 126
Isa 43:14-15 128
Isa 44:6 126
Isa 44:24 .... 126, 130
Isa 45:11-12 .... 126, 130
Isa 45:23 127
Isa 46:4 .... 58, 126
Isa 48:12 126

Isa 49:26 126
Isa 54:5 126
Isa 62:5 126
Isa 66:2 .... 126, 130

Jeremiah

Jer 3:1-2 126
Jer 23:5-6 128
Jer 46:10 129

Ezekiel

Ezek 30:3 129
Ezek 34:11-16 127

Hosea

Hos 2:16 126
Hos 11:9 128
Hos 13:4 .... 58, 126
Hos 13:14 127

Joel

Joel 1:15 129
Joel 2:32 128

Obadiah

Obad 1:15 129

Micah

Mic 5:2 119

Habakkuk

Hab 1:12............................ 128

Zephaniah

Zeph 1:7,14....................... 129
Zeph 3:9............................ 128

Zechariah

Zech 12:10 126

Zech 13:8-9....................... 128
Zech 14:5 129

Malachi

Mal 3:1.............................. 127
Mal 4:5.............................. 129

New Testament

Matthew

Matt 3:3,11-12 127
Matt 3:17 58
Matt 4:1,7 70
Matt 4:7 129
Matt 5:48 38
Matt 6:6-13 133
Matt 7:2 9
Matt 7:12 17
Matt 8:23-27 129
Matt 11:10 127
Matt 11:27 .... 82, 131
Matt 14:25-33 129
Matt 16:27 ..... 82, 83, 127, 185
Matt 17:5 58
Matt 19:27-29 86
Matt 19:28 .... 82, 83, 131
Matt 20:28 .... 73, 74
Matt 23:34 127
Matt 23:37-38 128
Matt 24:30 .... 82, 181
Matt 25:31 82
Matt 25:31-34,41,46 83
Matt 25:40,45 17
Matt 26:28 74
Matt 26:64 82
Matt 27:46 139
Matt 28:5-7 78
Matt 28:8-9 171
Matt 28:9 78
Matt 28:18 .... 82, 131

Mark

Mark 1:24 128
Mark 1:34 71
Mark 3:11-12 71
Mark 6:48-51 129
Mark 8:34 66
Mark 12:31 17
Mark 13:13 87
Mark 14:62 82
Mark 15:34 .... 138, 139
Mark 16:9 78
Mark 16:19 82

Luke

Luke 1:76 127
Luke 2:11 126
Luke 3:4-6 127
Luke 4:41 .... 71, 162
Luke 5:34-35 126

Luke 7:27 127
Luke 10:16 133
Luke 12:32 87
Luke 12:40 82
Luke 12:44 87
Luke 13:34-35 128
Luke 22:15-16,19-20,42-44 74
Luke 22:29-30 87
Luke 22:42-44 .... 73, 162
Luke 22:69 82
Luke 24:3-8 .... 78, 170
Luke 24:36-51 .... 78, 173

John

John 1:1 .... 58, 70, 108, 140
John 1:1,3,10,14 126
John 1:1-3,10,14 .... 57, 107
John 1:3 66
John 1:3,10,14 .... 34, 66, 109, 130, 147
John 1:6-8,15-36 127
John 1:10 .... 66, 149
John 1:12-13 .... 39, 66, 86
John 1:14 .... 58, 70, 152
John 1:18 .... 115, 127
John 3:13,31-32 58
John 3:15-16,36 .... 86, 188

John 3:16 .... 70, 136
John 3:16,18,35 58
John 3:16-17 58
John 3:31-32 122
John 3:35 .... 82, 131, 180
John 5:17-18 .... 62, 133, 143
John 5:22 127
John 5:22-30 83
John 5:23 .... 62, 133, 143
John 5:26 115
John 5:28-29 .... 78, 176, 183
John 6:19-21 129
John 6:32,38-40,44,46,57 58
John 6:33,38,41-42,50-51, 58,62 58
John 6:33,38,50-51,58,62 .. 122
John 6:40,47, 51,54-58 86
John 6:56 86
John 7:33-34 .... 58, 123
John 8:18,42 58
John 8:23 58
John 8:24,28 126
John 8:24,28,58 58
John 8:42 123
John 8:58 126
John 8:58-59 125
John 10:14-16 127

John 10:15 70
John 10:15,17-18 74
John 10:28 86
John 10:30 .... 62, 141
John 10:33 62
John 10:36 58
John 10:38 .... 61, 62, 137
John 12:39-41 127
John 12:41-50 58
John 12:45 62
John 13:3 .... 58, 82, 131, 180
John 13:19 .... 58, 126
John 13:31-32 .... 62, 81, 142
John 13:34 17
John 14:6 .... 82, 132, 179
John 14:7-12 62
John 14:9-11 145
John 14:10-11,20 ..... 6, 61, 62, 137, 141
John 14:13-14 133
John 14:16 .... 62, 144
John 14:20,23 .... 86, 193
John 14:28 144
John 15:1-11 .... 86, 139
John 15:10 .... 86, 188
John 15:23-24 133
John 16:5 58

John 16:15 .... 82, 131
John 16:23-24 133
John 16:26 .... 62, 144
John 16:28 58
John 17:1-2,5,24 81
John 17:2-3 86
John 17:3,8,21, 23, 25 58
John 17:5,22,24 .... 58, 120
John 17:9,15,20 62
John 17:10 .... 82, 131
John 17:11,21-22 62
John 17:11,21-23 .... 86, 139, 142, 146, 193
John 17:19 74
John 17:21,23 .... 61, 62, 137
John 17:22 .... 87, 195
John 18:5-8 .... 58, 126
John 19:34-37 126
John 20:19-20 78
John 20:25-29 78
John 20:28 116

Acts

Acts 1:1-11 78
Acts 1:9-11 82
Acts 2:20 129
Acts 2:32-33 .... 81, 82
Acts 3:14 128

Acts 3:20 .... 58, 121
Acts 4:10-12 .... 58, 82, 126, 128, 132, 179
Acts 7:55-56 .... 82, 137
Acts 7:59 .... 128, 130
Acts 9:5,13-14,17,21 128
Acts 10:36 .... 82, 131
Acts 10:42 83
Acts 13:37 78
Acts 17:31 .... 78, 83
Acts 20:28 116
Acts 20:32 .... 39, 86
Acts 24:15 ..... 78, 83, 176, 183
Acts 26:18 .... 39, 86
Acts 26:23 .... 73, 78

Romans

Rom 1:3 70
Rom 1:5 86
Rom 3:23-25 .... 73, 74
Rom 5:2 .... 87, 195
Rom 5:6-8 .... 74, 166
Rom 5:9-11 74
Rom 5:15-18 78
Rom 5:21 86
Rom 6:3-8 168
Rom 6:3-11 74
Rom 6:9-10 ... 70, 78, 159, 175
Rom 6:10 70
Rom 6:16 86
Rom 6:23 86
Rom 7:4 74
Rom 8:3 .... 58, 70, 156
Rom 8:3,32 136
Rom 8:9-11 86
Rom 8:14-21 .... 39, 86, 192
Rom 8:15,22-23 .... 39, 86, 189
Rom 8:16-17 86
Rom 8:17 .... 74, 195
Rom 8:17-21,28-30 87
Rom 8:19-21 .... 83, 186
Rom 8:28-30 87
Rom 8:32 .... 73, 74, 87
Rom 8:34 .... 70, 78, 82
Rom 9:5 .... 82, 116, 131
Rom 9:23-24 87
Rom 9:33 128
Rom 10:9,13 128
Rom 10:9-10 66
Rom 16:26 .... 86, 188

1 Corinthians

1 Cor 1:2 128
1 Cor 1:7-8 129
1 Cor 1:9 87

1 Cor 1:30 128
1 Cor 3:16-17 86
1 Cor 3:21-23 87
1 Cor 5:5 129
1 Cor 6:17 .... 86, 194
1 Cor 8:6 .... 34, 65, 66, 115, 130, 146, 150
1 Cor 10:1-4 128
1 Cor 10:9 129
1 Cor 15:4,12-26 78
1 Cor 15:5-8 78
1 Cor 15:6 171
1 Cor 15:12-30 .... 78, 83, 185
1 Cor 15:20,23 .... 78, 173
1 Cor 15:20-22 127
1 Cor 15:21 .... 70, 156
1 Cor 15:22 176
1 Cor 15:23 82
1 Cor 15:25-28 .... 82, 131
1 Cor 15:26 .... 78, 174
1 Cor 15:35,40-57 78
1 Cor 15:47 58
1 Cor 15:48-49 87

2 Corinthians

2 Cor 1:14 129
2 Cor 3:18 .... 87, 194
2 Cor 4:4 118
2 Cor 4:4-6 62
2 Cor 4:14 74
2 Cor 4:17 .... 87, 196
2 Cor 5:10 .... 83, 127, 185
2 Cor 5:14-15 74
2 Cor 5:15 .... 70, 78
2 Cor 5:19 .... 61, 62
2 Cor 5:21 70
2 Cor 6:10 87
2 Cor 8:9 .... 87, 114
2 Cor 9:7 66

Galatians

Gal 1:4 .... 73, 74
Gal 2:20 86
Gal 2:20-21 74
Gal 3:13 .... 74, 126
Gal 3:26-29 86
Gal 3:26-4:7 .... 39, 86, 190
Gal 3:28 17
Gal 4:4 .... 58, 70
Gal 5:1,13 .... 66, 151

Ephesians

Eph 1:4 86
Eph 1:4-5 .... 39, 86, 190
Eph 1:7 .... 74, 126
Eph 1:10,20-23 .... 82, 131

Eph 1:11-18............. 39, 86, 87
Eph 1:20....................... 78, 82
Eph 1:21............................. 81
Eph 2:5-6............................ 74
Eph 2:5-7..................... 87, 197
Eph 2:13-16........................ 74
Eph 3:19............................. 87
Eph 4:9-10......................... 58
Eph 4:13,15,24 .... 87, 195
Eph 5:20........................... 133

Philippians

Phil 2:5-7........................... 58
Phil 2:5-11................. 110, 157
Phil 2:6-8........................... 58
Phil 2:7-8........................... 70
Phil 2:9........................... 177
Phil 2:9-11............. 81, 82, 178
Phil 2:10-11..................... 127
Phil 3:10............................ 74

Colossians

Col 1:12-13................... 39, 86
Col 1:12-22..................... 111
Col 1:13-14..................... 126
Col 1:13-17.... 34, 66, 126, 130
Col 1:15..................... 62, 140
Col 1:15-16..................... 147

Col 1:15-17................. 57, 107
Col 1:16................. 66, 94, 150
Col 1:16-17..................... 94, 95
Col 1:16-20................. 82, 131
Col 1:17......... 66, 95, 129, 148
Col 1:18............................. 78
Col 1:19....... 62, 145, 152, 160
Col 1:20-22............. 70, 74, 166
Col 1:27...................... 86, 87
Col 2:9......... 62, 145, 152, 160
Col 2:9-10........................... 87
Col 2:14............................. 74
Col 3:1............................... 82
Col 3:4......................... 82, 87
Col 3:10............................. 87
Col 3:17........................... 133
Col 3:24........................ 39, 86

1 Thessalonians

1 Thes 2:12......................... 87
1 Thes 3:13................. 82, 129
1 Thes 4:14......................... 78
1 Thes 4:14-17 82
1 Thes 4:16....................... 129
1 Thes 5:2......................... 129
1 Thes 5:9-10 .... 74, 82

2 Thessalonians

2 Thes 1:7 181

2 Thes 1:7-10 82

2 Thes 1:12 116

2 Thes 2:8 .... 82, 128

2 Thes 2:13-14 87

2 Thes 4:14-17 182

1 Timothy

1 Tim 2:5 .... 82, 132

1 Tim 2:6 .... 73, 74, 165

1 Tim 6:14 .... 82, 129

1 Tim 6:14-15 127

2 Timothy

2 Tim 1:9-10 57

2 Tim 1:10 78

2 Tim 2:8 .... 78, 171

2 Tim 2:10 87

2 Tim 2:11 .... 74, 168

2 Tim 2:12 .... 87, 196

2 Tim 4:1 .... 83, 129

2 Tim 4:1,8 82

2 Tim 4:7-8 87

Titus

Tit 2:13 .... 82, 117, 129

Tit 2:13-14 126

Tit 2:14 .... 73, 74

Tit 3:7 .... 39, 86

Hebrews

Heb 1:2 .... 82, 131, 180

Heb 1:2-3 .... 34, 58, 62, 65, 70, 114, 130, 140

Heb 1:3 .... 66, 129, 133, 143, 148

Heb 1:5 58

Heb 1:6 130

Heb 1:8-9 130

Heb 1:8-10 .... 34, 66, 109, 130

Heb 1:10 126

Heb 1:10-12 .... 83, 130

Heb 1:13 82

Heb 1:14 .... 39, 86

Heb 2:9 .... 81, 177

Heb 2:9-10 .... 74, 163

Heb 2:10 ... 34, 66, 82, 87, 130, 131

Heb 2:10-17 .... 39, 86

Heb 2:14-17 .... 70, 154

Heb 2:14-18 .... 70, 156

Heb 2:18 70

Heb 3:14 .... 87, 196

Heb 4:15 .... 70, 158

Heb 5:7-9 73

Heb 5:9 .... 86, 188
Heb 7:25-28 74
Heb 7:26 .... 70, 81
Heb 7:27 70
Heb 8:1 82
Heb 9:11-14 74
Heb 9:11-28 74
Heb 9:12,25-28 70
Heb 9:14 70
Heb 9:15 .... 39, 86
Heb 9:15,26-28 74
Heb 9:28 82
Heb 10:10-14 .... 70, 160
Heb 10:10-20 .... 73, 74
Heb 10:12 82
Heb 12:2 82
Heb 12:9-10 87

James

Jas 1:12 87
Jas 2:5 .... 39, 86, 87

1 Peter

1 Pet 1:2 86
1 Pet 1:3-5 .... 39, 86
1 Pet 1:11,18-20 .... 73, 74, 164
1 Pet 1:13-14,22-23 86
1 Pet 1:18-20 .... 74, 121

1 Pet 1:19-20 57
1 Pet 1:20 58
1 Pet 2:4-8 128
1 Pet 2:21-24 .... 73, 74, 163
1 Pet 2:22 70
1 Pet 2:24 74
1 Pet 2:25 127
1 Pet 3:18 .... 70, 74
1 Pet 3:18-20 .... 78, 169
1 Pet 3:21 78
1 Pet 3:21-22 178
1 Pet 3:22 .... 81, 82
1 Pet 4:5-6 83
1 Pet 4:6 169
1 Pet 5:4 .... 82, 127
1 Pet 5:10 86

2 Peter

2 Pet 1:1 117
2 Pet 1:3-4 .... 87, 194
2 Pet 1:17 .... 58, 81
2 Pet 3:10 129
2 Pet 3:10-13 .... 83, 186

1 John

1 Jn 1:1-2 .... 57, 70
1 Jn 1:2 86
1 Jn 1:3-7 87

1 Jn 1:7 .... 74, 167

1 Jn 2:13 57

1 Jn 2:20 128

1 Jn 2:23 133

1 Jn 2:25 86

1 Jn 2:29-3:3 ..... 39, 86, 87, 191

1 Jn 3:5 70

1 Jn 3:9 .... 39, 86

1 Jn 4:2-3 .... 70, 152, 159

1 Jn 4:9-10 .... 58, 136

1 Jn 4:9-10,14 ... 58, 73, 74, 165

1 Jn 4:14 58

1 Jn 4:14-15 126

1 Jn 4:16-17 .... 9, 27

1 Jn 5:1-5 .... 39, 86

1 Jn 5:3 86

1 Jn 5:9-13,20 86

1 Jn 5:20 .... 86, 117

2 John

2 Jn 1:4,6 86

2 Jn 1:7 .... 70, 152, 159

Jude

Jude 1:14 .... 82, 129

Jude 1:21 86

Revelation

Rev 1:5 .... 74, 78

Rev 1:6 .... 87, 197

Rev 1:7 126

Rev 1:8,17-18 126

Rev 1:18 .... 78, 83, 174

Rev 3:14 .... 34, 65, 130

Rev 3:20 66

Rev 3:21 .... 87, 196

Rev 5:5,9,12 70

Rev 5:5,9,12-13 81

Rev 5:9 74

Rev 5:10 87

Rev 5:13-14 82

Rev 7:17 .... 82, 132

Rev 17:14 .... 58, 127

Rev 19:7-8 126

Rev 19:13-16 .... 58, 127

Rev 20:10-15 83

Rev 20:4 87

Rev 20:11 83

Rev 20:13-14 .... 78, 174

Rev 21:1 186

Rev 21:1,5 83

Rev 21:7 .... 39, 86, 87, 192

Rev 21:9 126

Rev 22:5 87

Rev 22:6,16 118

Rev 22:12 .... 82, 83

Rev 22:12-16 126

Rev 22:20 128

INDEX

Abiogenesis 98

Act, do not be content to be acted upon 48, 93

Americans 14, 15

Anglican/Independent Catholic 40

Atheism 19, 46, 51, 96, 97, 98, 101, 200

Baha'i, the 104

Behavior is always more important than interpretation 7, 9

Benjamin Franklin 16

Big Bang 97, 106

Biologists 98

Bodily self-control 18

Brain drain 21

Buddhism 104

Canada 20

Capitalism 4, 14

Carbohydrates

   Components of a living cell 98

Cause of anatomically modern humans

   Empirical evidence for God 99

Cause of life

   Empirical evidence for God 98

Cause of the New Testament's coherent cosmology

   Empirical evidence for God 102, 103

Cause of the universe

   Empirical evidence for God 97

Charity 18, 49

Children of God, The 33, 39, 48, 49, 156, 187, 191, 192, 193, 194, 195, 196, 197, 200

   Are adopted by the Father 33, 39, 50, 189, 192, 201

   Become God's heirs and fellow-heirs with Christ 39, 49, 50, 131, 190, 191, 192, 195, 196, 197, 199

   Share God's glory ... 50, 195

217

Share in God's nature as "God"....33, 50, 194, 200

Share in God's oneness and mutual indwelling.....49, 50, 131, 139, 141, 142, 146, 193, 200

Will reign over the universe beneath Christ's dominion......................39

Christ's Golden Rule........ 19, 22

Christ's moral teachings.......13, 18, 21, 22, 24, 104

Christian ethics 17, 18, 21

Christian morality

Creates an artificial floor..............................20

Christian worldview 13

Christianity changed the world................................ 3

Christianity's five branches......................... 40

Core hymns 4

Correlative anthology 46, 49, 102, 199

Cosmology....45, 46, 106, 147

Critics think they can tell God what to do........... 8, 9

Dark energy....................... 97

Dark matter 97

Death

Comes for all of us...........48

Is unpredictable...............48

Eastern Christian 40

Emancipation of the slaves................................15

Empathetic morality ...17, 25

Empirical evidence for God...47, 48, 52, 96, 97, 99, 199

Endure to the end.........4, 51, 196, 201

England............................105

Enzymes............................98

Epilogue hymn 4

Eternal Life 38, 105, 187, 201

Europe...................13, 14, 104

Europeans..........................15

Expressed doctrine does not change...................5, 6

Face value is official doctrine

Scripture text's..............5, 6

Fall, The 34, 121

Fine-tuned universe 148

Follow Christ no matter what 31, 38, 49, 50, 187

Four sigma level of evidence........................103

INDEX | 219

France 105

Freedom of thought

The most basic of rights 8

General relativity 97

George Washington 16

Germany 105

God cares about what you become during your lifetime 7

God does not care for what is in your head 7

God made you free 9

Gratitude 26, 177, 178

Hard path

Choose the 4

Harmonizing editor ... 42, 43, 46, 47, 52, 101, 102, 103, 199

Hinduism 104

Holy Bible

Credibility of 4, 48

Holy Bible, The

Objective evidence for its credibility 41, 43, 47, 48, 52

Subjective evidence for its credibility 40, 41, 48

Holy Spirit, The 3, 38, 40, 48, 49, 51, 199, 200

Dwells within the Christian 38, 40, 51

Provides a subjective witness of the Truth 40, 48

Testifies of the Son of God 3, 40

Homo sapiens sapiens 99, 100, 107

Human dignity 17, 20, 26

Human equality ... 17, 20, 21, 23, 24, 26, 110, 120, 133, 143, 157

Innate moral rights 19, 23, 24, 133

Internal desire to triumph over others 19

Interpretation

Dangerous to insist one must agree on a specific interpretation to be saved 5, 8, 9

It is fine to understand a passage differently ... 5, 7, 9

Interpretation is subjective 5, 6, 8

Islam 104

James Madison 16

Jesus Christ

"God" by nature 34

Annulled the Fall ... 34, 167

Atonement of 2, 34, 35, 36, 37, 38, 39, 51, 121,

131, 156, 160, 162, 163, 169, 176, 177, 199

Atonement was infinite..*33, 34, 35, 39, 97, 163, 176*

Atonement was the most important event in the history of the universe *4, 34, 39, 169*

Became human flesh.....*152, 154, 155, 156, 167, 177, 200*

Conjoined the God and human natures together *33, 34*

Controls death and Hades *169, 174*

Created the universe..........*1, 31, 32, 34, 96, 106, 130, 131, 140, 146, 147, 149, 150, 151, 157*

Credibility of *4, 48*

Death of................*31, 33, 51*

Died for humanity.........*165*

Equal to the Father........*143*

Exact duplicate of the Father........................*140*

Foreordained before the Earth was made....................*121*

Gatekeeper *132*

Gave up his glory to become human *1, 120*

Gives the gift of physical immortality to all...*2, 33, 175, 178, 182, 187*

God's fulness was in his body *144, 153, 160*

Greatest of all *49, 177*

Has an immortal physical body *161, 171, 173*

His name is above all names *177*

Humbled himself to become human.....................*1, 31*

Humility of *157*

Infinite Atonement annuls the Fall *33, 38*

Infinite scope of his Atonement *2, 34, 35, 131, 163, 199*

Inherits the universe *32, 33, 49, 50, 131, 140, 163, 169, 180, 196, 197*

Is "God" by nature *120, 131*

Is Jehovah or Yahweh (YHWH)..*125, 131, 133, 134*

Is our God *13, 32, 34, 49, 51, 52, 133, 200, 201*

Is our Lord and Savior ...*52, 131*

Is the Son of Jehovah or Yahweh (YHWH) *135*

Joy in 10

Judge......... 6, 7, 8, 9, 30, 32, 33, 182, 185

Judges all humanity 49, 131, 183

Keeps the forces of the universe together 32, 140, 143, 148

Most influential person in history 1, 13, 24, 199

One-time mortality of 158

One-time sacrifice of 160

Only way to salvation ... 40, 48, 51, 180

Only way to the Father 33, 179

Preached to the dead in Hades 168

Resurrection of 36, 49, 156, 160, 168, 169, 171, 177

Returns with angels 3

Second Coming of 3, 161, 181, 182, 185

Shares all he has with his followers 4, 33, 196, 197

Single incarnation 158, 175

Sinlessness of 155

Son of God, The 3, 32, 47, 48, 120, 123, 124, 133, 134, 149, 152, 159, 162, 168, 194, 201

Source of the West's ethics 104

Suffered infinite pain 33, 35, 162, 163

Suffered infinite terror ... 35

Suffering of 2

The Father's Only Begotten Son 40, 51, 135, 146, 200

Took upon himself the consequences of our sins 2

World's debt to 14, 18, 26, 49, 103, 104, 105, 199

Keep God's commandments 3, 7, 27-30, 50, 188, 200

Koine Greek............. 108, 144

Latter-day Saint............. 2, 40

Lens

   Theological 5

Lipids

   Components of a living cell 98

Love God 2, 7, 29, 50, 200

Love your neighbor 3, 7, 17, 29, 50, 200

Love yourself...... 3, 7, 29, 50, 200

Meaningful life

   The best life 2, 4, 26, 106, 201

Mecca 104

Might makes right 20

Modern Science, Technology, Engineering, and Mathematics (STEM) 4, 14, 25

Moral discipline 18, 151

Moral principles 17, 20

Mutual indwelling 6, 50, 136, 138, 141, 142, 193, 200

Natural rights 4, 13, 14, 15, 16, 17, 20, 21, 23, 25, 26, 104, 105

   Are reciprocal 13, 20

   Justification comes from Christ's moral teachings 18, 19, 20, 21, 23

Neoplatonism 139

Nestle-Aland 28 .... 93, 108

New Testament 41, 42, 43, 46, 47, 48, 49, 51, 52, 93, 101, 102, 103, 108, 124, 125, 130, 133, 134, 135, 144, 199

New Testament, The

   Did not have a common frame nor harmonizing editor 42, 47, 52, 101, 102, 103

   Has a single coherent cosmology 33, 41, 43, 103

   Is a correlative anthology 41, 42, 102, 103

North America 13, 14, 104

Nucleic acids

   Components of a living cell 98

Objective evidence 47

Official doctrine is different from interpretation 5, 6

Pedophilia

   One of the worst evils 24

Physical immortality 37, 50, 153, 155, 160, 161, 169, 173, 175, 178, 181, 182, 183, 186, 187, 199

Powerful insiders are more valuable than weak outsiders 19, 20, 23

Prebiotic Earth 98, 149

Prologue hymn 4

Proteins

   Components of a living cell 98

Protestant 40

Quantum field theory 97

Quantum fluctuation 97

Reciprocal morality 20

Repentance...... 38, 48, 50, 51, 187, 188, 200

Representative government 4, 14

Richard Wurmbrand 26

Roman Catholic................. 40

Rome................................ 104

Rule of law, The 4, 14, 21

Salt Lake City 104

Scientific Method 105

Sense of group identity

Responsible for most violence and death.................... 19

Shintoism 104

Sikhism.............................. 104

Sing the hymns......... 3, 10, 52

Slavery................................ 24

Social Contract 13, 21

Son of Jehovah.................. 124

Spacetime........................... 97

Spain................................. 105

Strive to obey Christ no matter what 33, 37, 38, 49, 50, 187, 188

Synthetic chemists 98

Taoism 104

Temple of God

Your body is a.................. 29

The Father, Son, and Holy Spirit

Are One God and share a common space 136

Thomas Jefferson 16

Trinity.............................. 138

True biblical doctrines........ 1, 2, 3, 93

Tyranny................ 20, 24, 104

United States 20, 105

US Civil War...................... 15

US Constitution................. 14

US Founding Fathers.. 16, 17

Viktor Frankl 26

We will not receive charity when judged if we lack charity to others.... 8, 9, 10

Western civilization... 15, 19, 20, 25

Built on Christian morality.........21, 24, 104

Framers of 14, 22

Western ethics 21

Women

Historical status of......... 24

Word of God

Strengthens us 3

Worst enemy, Your
Has the same natural rights you have 20

YHWH 124, 131

You will be judged with the same standard that you judge others 9

ABOUT THE AUTHOR

Edward K. Watson has over 70,000 hours in writing, editing, and analyzing complex documents such as RFPs, proposals, and project execution plans for very large projects, including a dozen in the billion-dollar range. He is the author of the four-volume *Is Jesus "God"? A Witness to the World That Jesus is the Christ, the Eternal God*. The work details the only empirical evidence that anyone can use to justify the belief that the Holy Bible is inspired by God (*the New Testament is a frameless, unharmonized, correlative anthology*). The book also provides three additional pieces of evidence that support belief in God and demolishes atheism.

He published his first book in 1998 (***Mormonism***), but lost interest in Latter-day Saint apologetics and discontinued the series. After a decade as an atheist, he is, once again, a devout member of the Church of Jesus Christ of Latter-day Saints and has enormous appreciation for the teachings in the Book of Mormon concerning our God, Jesus Christ, and of his infinite Atonement.

Ed defends Christianity as a whole and supports the faith of all Christians regardless of their church. He prefers to build bridges rather than destroy homes. He found Jesus in his church and recognizes others find Him in different churches. Ed does not concern himself with arguments concerning biblical interpretation since he recognizes that those who insist others must believe their interpretation of specific text to be saved usurp Christ's judgment authority over us. *If God never said we must interpret a passage in a specific way to be saved, then no one else can either*. Christ, alone, decides our eternal fate. Those who condemn others to eternal torture in hell for not believing the same thing they do will be accountable for their uncharitable actions. He takes Christ's words seriously:

> *You will be judged with the same standard that you judge others; you will be measured with the same measure you use on others. (Matthew 7:2)*

It only took thirty years, thousands of books, and tens of thousands of dollars, but Ed is finally starting to understand that what is truly important in life is not what he knows, but who he is as a person. He finally gets what the Savior said when he told us to:

- LOVE GOD
- LOVE YOUR NEIGHBOR
- LOVE YOURSELF
- KEEP THE COMMANDMENTS

To be truly wise and content means to live a life of meaning, where we genuinely love. We can then leave this world with joy, knowing that as God is, so are we (1 John 4:16-17).

www.ingramcontent.com/pod-product-compliance
Lightning Source LLC
Chambersburg PA
CBHW072224200426

43209CB00073B/1933/J